Maurice Ravel, 1933 (Lipnitzki).

MAURICE RAVEL

by
ROLAND-MANUEL

Translated from the French by
CYNTHIA JOLLY

41277

Dover Publications, Inc.
New York

This Dover edition, first published in 1972, is a republication of the English translation originally published by Dennis Dobson, London, in 1947. The text is complete and unabridged, except that the discography has been deleted because it has been superseded by up-to-date and readily available catalogs of recordings.

This edition is published through special arrangement with Dobson Books, Ltd., 80 Kensington Church St., London W 8, publisher of the original English edition.

International Standard Book Number: 0-486-20695-5
Library of Congress Catalog Card Number: 76-186313

Manufactured in the United States of America
Dover Publications, Inc.
180 Varick Street
New York, N. Y. 10014

INTRODUCTION BY THE EDITOR

The writer of this book has more than one claim upon our attention, as he traces the main outlines of Ravel's life and work. M. Roland-Manuel is in the fortunate position of knowing more about both of these matters than anyone else, at least since the death of Calvocoressi. He was a friend (presumably one of the small band of intimates) of Ravel and also a pupil. He is therefore able, as few now are, to speak with equal authority of the man and the musician.

Neither will have been easy to delineate. Ravel mistrusted the mob and had no illusions about the value of factitious publicity in the gossip-press. He started as a young man with what seems like an attempt to put up a material façade (fastidious apparel, that and other attributes of Baudelaire's dandy) behind which he could withdraw to concentrate on the work in hand. He ended by having created a more subtle defence, an outer integument of social charm that masked the inner self. Of that self Ravel was intensely and increasingly aware. Elsewhere M. Roland-Manuel has written of the detachment Ravel attained from his social graces; he had become critic of his own act. In the same way he reached a point from which he watched no longer himself but his self. It may well be that he never became involved; nothing in the present study suggests exclusive introspection. He was profoundly and precisely interested. One imagines him perfecting a technique of living with as much application as he brought to his other technique, music. In both cases the processes were withheld from the gaze of the world. Hence the difficulty of biography and critical judgment even in the case of a privileged observer such as M. Roland-Manuel.

The music of Ravel, its exterior as deceptive as that of the musician himself, has led many to suppose that it is a cold void in which their personal vision could not exist. Undoubtedly he reached in his later works a much rarefied refinement, too abstract to please those who had been satisfied with "Ma mère l'oye." There seemed to be something lost; a link had dropped out of the chain. M. Roland-Manuel's pages show that this was not so. What seemed contradictions were logical reactions. The line of development is unbroken from the Habanera of 1895 to the Piano Concertos published in 1931. In the present volumes the steps which led from the early work to the late, by way of works seemingly so far removed as the Bolero, are made evident in a way which should interest an enquirer and stimulate a student to further research.

SCOTT GODDARD

Maurice Ravel in 1879 with his parents (Edouard Ravel).

CONTENTS

LIST OF ILLUSTRATIONS

9

LIST OF ILLUSTRATIONS—*continued.*

AUTHOR'S PREFACE

IN THE PAGES THAT FOLLOW I HAVE TRIED TO DESCRIBE AS accurately and objectively as possible the chief characteristics of Maurice Ravel's life and work.

The first book is taken up with a biography of the composer. I have endeavoured to trace the development of his personality in relation to the course of events, showing as I do so the genesis and distinctive character of each work.

His style and technique are considered in a more general study which occupies the first chapter of the second book. In the last chapter I have tried to give in outline a portrait of the man and the artist.

" To the dead we owe but the truth." The intimate friends of a famous man often hesitate to make any public statement about him immediately after his death. Indeed, whether they disguise or disclose what they know, they run the risk of appearing unworthy either of their task or their friend. If I have not been guilty of such hesitation, it is because everything about Maurice Ravel is a delight to describe, except the grief of having lost him. For although he was a man of such fastidious reserve, he had no secret but the secret of his genius.

Accuracy and sincerity have been made easier for me, in that the relations and friends of the master, who have nothing to conceal, have freely given me their help in completing or correcting my reminiscences. It would be impossible to thank them all ; but I cannot fail to mention some few in recognition of their share in this book : MM. Edouard Ravel and Alfred Perrin, the composer's brother and cousin ; Maurice Delage, Lucien Garban, Manuel Rosenthal, Léon Leyritz, René Dommange ; Mmes Hélène Jourdan-Morhange and Marguerite Long ; Mlle Marie Gaudin ; the Professors Pasteur Vallery-Radot, Alajouanine and Clovis Vincent.

R. M.

Joseph Ravel and his two sons (Maurice on right) about 1884.

PART ONE

CHAPTER I

*Joseph Ravel—his family origins—his stay in Spain—a meeting at Aranjuez—marriage of Joseph Ravel and Marie Delouart—birth of Maurice Ravel—the Basque character—Basque music—*España de panderetas.

IN PARIS IN 1868 THERE LIVED A YOUNG AND EXCEPTIONALLY cultured engineer with an alert and enquiring mind. Pierre-Joseph Ravel was one of those learned research-workers whose strength of mind is combined with modesty, and who, always spurred on by new problems, have only one ambition, to solve the difficulties which face them, and often only one reward, the satisfaction of having done so. Such disinterested inventors may be found at the beginning of all great industrial achievements, but industry is too preoccupied to recall the worth of those pioneers who have served it in its early stages. So we find that only technical reviews have recognized and honoured Joseph Ravel as one of the real pioneers of the motor industry, the first builder of a " steam generator, fired by mineral oils, applied to locomotion,"[1] and, later on, the inventor of a two-stroke super-charged engine.

Joseph Ravel, born in 1832, originally came from Versoix, a little market town on the Lake of Geneva, which, by the terms of the 1815 treaty, was restored to the canton of Geneva. Documents brought to my notice by M. Alfred Perrin, the composer's first cousin, confirm the statement of the *Dictionnaire historique et biographique de la Suisse*, to the effect that the Ravel family originated in Collonges-sous-Salève, a village of Haute-Savoie.

Aimé (or Ami) Ravel,[2] who was born at Collonges in 1800, came to Versoix, where he became a baker. He acquired

---

[1] Patent No. 82263 J.R. dated the 2nd September, 1868. Pierre Souvestre vouches for a motor vehicle built by Joseph Ravel and heated by this method which, driven by the inventor, travelled to and fro in two hours along the Rue de la Révolte during the winter of 1868.

[2] The spelling of the name has undergone various important modifications in the course of copying into parish registers ; the father of Aimé Ravel was called François *Ravex* when his son was baptized, François *Ravet* four years later in the

13

Swiss nationality in 1834. He married a young Swiss girl called Caroline Grosfort, and had five children—Joseph, the engineer, and later the father of Maurice Ravel, Marie, Alexandrine, Louise and Edouard.

Joseph Ravel, a sensitive and reserved character of great charm, was brought into contact with the artistic world by his younger brother Edouard, a painter of some repute, whose canvases and decorative panels may be seen at Geneva, Lausanne and Neuchâtel, as well as in the art galleries at Marseille and Lille. Joseph Ravel also was sufficiently interested in music to have begun to study. In a word, he was a civilized man, alive to the most daring flights of thought and sensitive to every trend of creative imagination.

Shortly after the war of 1870, he was summoned to Spain to assist in the building of railways. At New Castille, in 1873, he met the girl he was to marry. Maurice Ravel places the first meeting of his parents in the leafy shades of Aranjuez. It would be pleasant if truth could join hands with fantasy at this point ; if some overwhelming destiny had chosen the garden of the " Ile," there to link the lives of these two who were to be the parents of the composer of *Jeux d'eau*, the *Miroirs*, *L'Heure Espagnole* and *Le Tombeau de Couperin*. For this park in the French style, set like a fairy oasis in the centre of the Castillian desert, forms the most Ravelian landscape in the world, with its *alamedas*[3] and a palace still dreaming of Marie-Louise of Savoy and Domenico Scarlatti ; from the fountains the water of the Tagus gushes into the pools where

---

burial register at Collonges. Ravex, Ravet, or Ravez are patronymics of Savoy and are not affected by local pronunciation. The " l " of Ravel is obviously caused by a mistaken reading of " t."

The name, under these different spellings, is fairly common : a Simon Ravez, born at Rive-de-Gier in 1770, was a French peer under Charles X. Ravel is a character first made famous by a comic actor of Bordeaux, Pierre Alfred Ravel, whose buffoonery was sufficiently famous towards the end of last century to cause engravings of the " incomparable Ravel," and to provide the title of several revues, as though he were a typical character of the Commedia.

It is also worth noting that the same patronymic belongs to certain Jewish families ; in such cases Ravel is derived from " Rabbele "—a young rabbi—which gave rise in America and, recently, in Germany, to a belief in Ravel's semitic origins. Many proofs have been produced in support of this mistaken opinion ; especially the interest which Maurice Ravel took in Jewish matters, his harmonizations of Hebrew melodies, and, above all, the close friendships he formed with several Jewish people who were—and are—some of his finest interpreters and best friends.

[3] " Alamedas " : public walks shaded with trees. (Translator's note.)

14

the birds come to drink, close by a porcelain room whose ornamentation is rich in representations of an altogether fantastic Cathay.

To judge by her old portraits as well as by the gentle, refined features which were still hers under the lovely white hair of the last years of her life, Marie Delouart must have been a charming fiancée.   She was a Basque from the lower Pyrenees, and her name, though originally Deluarte or Eluarte, was gallicised on the French side of the mountains, and serves to make her nationality quite obvious.

Joseph Ravel and Marie Delouart were married in 1874, and lived for some time at Ciboure, a port on the Basque coast separated by the Nivelle from Saint-Jean-de-Luz. At No. 12, on the quayside of the Nivelle,[1] Joseph Maurice Ravel was born on the 7th March, 1875.   A few days later—on the 13th March —he was baptized by the priest of the parish of St. Vincent, the godparents being Simon Goyenague and Gracieuse Bilac, his maternal aunt.   Three months later, the Ravel family permanently settled in Paris.

When a biographer comes to consider the completed work and final destiny of an artist, it is obviously easy for him to draw up *a posteriori* his hero's horoscope, to deal as suits his purpose with questions of heredity or climate and to bring all this into line with the vital characteristics of the race. Certainly, both physically and intellectually, Maurice Ravel's Basque origin impressed itself in a peculiarly significant manner on his character.   To ignore it would be to neglect much which is essential to his character and genius.   But such influences must be seen in perspective ; it is fatally easy to confuse the Basque country with its neighbours.

Ravel's native country is the classic home of nimble wits, bold and stubborn pride and unswerving purpose.   Dancers, *pelotaris*, peasants, husbandmen and sailors are all sons of this land, small men with close-set eyes, who go uncompromisingly to their goals without allowing themselves to be distracted by the happenings about them.

When their American cousins see them from a distance, they recognize their ability to carry all enterprise through, but criticize them for wearing blinkers and seeing nothing above or

[1] Previously Rue du Quai ; since 1929, Quai Maurice Ravel.

beyond the goal they have set themselves. Certainly it is true enough that these adventurers never let go their life-line, and that the further they penetrate among unfamiliar ideas, the more tenaciously they cling to it. It follows that to the pursuit of quite insane schemes they apply the strictest orderliness, and use business tactics for the loftiest and most disinterested ends—even when it is a " matter of salvation."

It is not simply chance that two of the most famous specialists in this supreme problem should both have been born on the Cantabrian shore ; no mere chance that the father of the Jesuits and the oracle of the Jansenists—St. Ignatius Loyola and the abbé of Saint-Cyran—were blood brothers.

Both music and language distinguish the Basques from their neighbours. Basque folk-songs have their own modes and rhythms which resemble Breton music more than Spanish songs and dances. But Maurice Ravel did not know the *aurresku* and the *zortzicos* until he grew up. Even then he only heard them once. During his early childhood he was seldom lulled by his native airs, which were hardly, if at all, known by those about him.

The first songs hummed to him, which were to haunt him all his life, came from the mixture of treasure and dross produced by that racy and ill-famed part of Spain, which is called *España de panderetas*—the Spain that delights in the so-called " Tambour de Basque " ; the country of *boléros*, *sevillanos*, *guarjiras*, and also, of course, *habañeras* ; Andalusian and Cuban songs and dances grown languid, sugary and sophisticated from two centuries of Italian influence, and lastly, the refrains of the *zarzuelas* ; for the end of the last century saw the triumph of those delightful baroque operettas where the vulgar frivolity of the mandolines rivals the high seriousness of the mournful guitars—Neapolitan fantasies with " a dash of Spain."

Such was the music which the composer of *L'Heure Espagnole* breathed in with his native air, and his mother's voice infinitely prolonged its echoes as she rocked her spoilt child to sleep ; one day the artificial glitter of those Spanish ditties was to evoke a Spain of dreams and illusions, the Spain of Maurice Ravel.

CHAPTER II

Childhood and musical apprenticeship—his first teachers—Henri Ghys and Charles-René—1889: The Conservatoire and the Exhibition—Charles de Bériot—Ricardo Viñes—with Emile Pessard—Chabrier and Satie—first compositions.

IN JUNE, 1875, THE RAVEL FAMILY SETTLED IN PARIS, AT NO. 40, Rue des Martyrs, where Edward, the second son, was born three years later.

Joseph Ravel appears to have been an extremely gentle and patient teacher. Although he refused to give a definite direction to his children's studies, he played with the idea that one of them would become a musician. It so happened that this wish found fulfilment beyond his dreams, for he soon saw without any doubt that both his sons were extremely musical. After a thorough testing, he came to the conclusion that the more gifted of the two was the least keen to work ; for Maurice Ravel was always a tractable but nonchalant student.

" Even as a child," he said,[1] " I was sensitive to music—to all kinds of music. My father, who was infinitely better qualified than the majority of amateurs, knew how to develop my tastes and stimulate my interest at an early age." This stimulus took the form of an allowance of ten sous for each half-hour's effective piano-practice : a considerable amount of pocket-money for the time, painfully earned.

" Instead of notation, the theory of which I have never learned," Ravel goes on, " I began to study the piano at about six years of age. My first master was Henri Ghys . . . " Henri Ghys, the excellent musician of the *Air Louis XIII*, used to keep a diary, now piously preserved by his family, which fixes and comments upon this little event :

" 31st May, 1882. Today I began teaching a young pupil,

[1] Extract of a draft document which I took at Maurice Ravel's dictation, about the 15th October, 1928 (still unpublished, so far as I am aware) and intended to be a biographical sketch, at the request of a firm of pianola-makers. Subsequent borrowings from this document will be noted by a reference to " Biographical Sketch."

Maurice Ravel, who appears to be an intelligent boy. Evidently I'm now doomed to teach children."

Beginnings as simple as these are not those of an infant prodigy. The education of this young student was to progress wisely under good teachers, without haste or mishap.

1887 was a great year for French music. At the Opéra-Comique, the score of Emmanuel Chabrier's *Roi Malgré Lui* braved the footlights and justly escaped the flames (which destroyed the theatre). At Rome, in the silence of the " Etruscan tomb " at the Villa Medici, a young man of genius scored the first chords of *La Damoiselle Elue*. At Montmartre, Erik Satie, as " parcier " of " l'église métropolitaine d'art de Jésus Conducteur," escaped from a dwelling the size of a cupboard, and hurried off to try his extraordinary *Sarabandes* on the piano at the *Auberge du Clou*.

Maurice Ravel was now twelve years old, and as yet had had no contact with the world where the renaissance of French music was being prepared. All the same his new harmony teacher, Charles-René, continually drummed into his head the three inversions of the chord of the major seventh.

Charles-René, a disciple of Léo Delibes, whom he succeeded at the Conservatoire, was a clear-headed and well-informed teacher, and an excellent musician into the bargain. He used to invite his pupils to write short compositions in whatever form they liked, over and above their harmony exercises. Some variations on a *chorale* by Schumann and the first movement of a sonata, submitted by the pupil Ravel, made such an impression on the teacher that, twenty-five years later, he told Ravel's pupils that he was even then surprised by their perfect coherence and, even more, by the curious originality of their melodic line. In 1913 this master of so profound a judgement and so long a memory said, " He was writing essays in composition for me which were of real interest, and already revealed aspirations towards a refined, lofty and subtilized art, which now forms his noble and constant preoccupation. There has been an essential unity in his artistic development ; his conception of music is entirely spontaneous, and not the result of effort, as it is with so many others."

In 1889, at fourteen years old, Ravel was admitted to the Conservatoire as a pupil in Anthiome's class for preparatory

piano.   During the same year, he was allowed to visit the
World Exhibition, where the famous Rue de Caire did not hold
his attention so much as the Chinese shops and the Javanese
theatre.   The *gamelangs* were to him a revelation of the attraction of the gapped scales which form the essential fascination
of the music of the Far East.   The exotic melodies bewitched
and obsessed him, as they obsessed all composers who heard
them performed before European audiences for the first time.
Musicians crowded to hear these magic interludes, magic in
the true sense of the term, and their work shows the continued
influence of these performances.   Although as yet he did not
know them, the young Ravel rubbed shoulders with the artists
who were to inspire his early writing : Emmanuel Chabrier,
Claude Debussy, Erik Satie, and, of course, the admirable
Rimsky-Korsakov, who in his memoirs gracelessly confessed
it was this music that gave him the only pleasure he found in
Paris.

In 1891, armed with a medal, the first class for piano-playing,
the young Ravel was promoted to Charles de Bériot's class.
There he made friends with another pupil, Ricardo Viñes,
who was to become, and to remain, the most devoted, faithful,
and admirable interpreter of the composer's piano works.
Ravel felt at home in the class, where his best friend was a
Catalan from Lerida, and where his master also had connections with Spain—and romantic Spain at that—through
Malibran and Manuel Garcia.   Sixteen years later, the composer of the *Rapsodie espagnole* was to dedicate the work to " his
dear master Charles de Bériot."

During these formative years, Ravel showed himself a
good pupil who, though he certainly did not cram like an
examination fiend, on the other hand did not ape the impatient
genius who is irked by discipline and constantly quibbles with
School regulations.   Reared in the " Seraglio " it goes
without saying that he knew its labyrinthine ways, and even
its secret staircases.[1]   Convinced, like the Duchess Sanseverina
and Paul Valéry that " no one can be sceptical where the
principles of a technique are concerned," Emile Pessard's
harmony pupil was not keen so much to disobey Reber as to
expose Dubois in an act of liberalism.   He took malicious

[1] An allusion to Racine's *Bajazet*.   (Translator's note.)

19

pleasure in improving on his masters and examiners, which is not always the best way to their good graces. . . . One day he was to learn this to his cost.

Irony in a Conservatoire is not a good recommendation—and the less so when it appears under cover of a practised docility. What is more unnerving than strict conformity side by side with a love of freedom and daring which seems to contradict such extreme orthodoxy? It lays a man open to the accusation of affectation and preciosity by contemporaries not necessarily either cultured or well-mannered. From people like this were to be drawn later the band of embittered colleagues, whose ceaseless spite obstinately pursues great artists on the road to success.

A contrast, of course, is not always a contradiction. A liking for danger does not necessarily rule out a sense of discipline. In the case of the Basque Ravel, the latter is dominant. In pushing scholastic method to its farthest limits, the young Ravel asked no more of academic exercises than the suppleness and versatility they confer—in short, the means of independence. Ravel seems to have realized very quickly that a love of novelty and a spirit of adventure are valueless and lead nowhere if they overlook the real merits of a craftsmanship commensurate with their ambitions. That implies control which is only obtained by the exercise of technical skill.

While he was busy banishing fifths and octaves, the pupil of the innocuous Emile Pessard brought to the class, along with his harmony exercises, Emmanuel Chabrier's *Chanson pour Jeanne* and the unpublished *Gymnopédies* and *Sarabandes* of an equally unknown composer : Erik Satie. For he had just discovered these novelties and had been as fascinated by them as by the personalities of their creators.

Full of enthusiasm for the *Trois Valses Romantiques*, with their modal energy and unhampered dissonance, he decided to study them with Ricardo Viñes, and play them to Chabrier. Chabrier entertained his sixteen-year-old admirers in his inimitable way, lavishing on them all the fireworks of his gruff hospitality. Their performance let loose a flood of encouragement and invective, imperious and contradictory exhortations, which left the two interpreters fascinated but exhausted.

As for Satie, that mysterious and inaccessible character, it was Ravel's father, assuredly the most providential of guardians, who knew where to run him to earth in the *Nouvelle Athènes* café, at the table of the engraver Marcelin Desboutin. Maurice Ravel never tired of emphasizing the decisive character of this meeting with Satie. The advice, the devilment, the artless audacity of that wierd Socrates inspired, whether one likes it or not, very many of the technical achievements and triumphs of æsthetic judgement for which his successors justifiably gain the credit ; such achievements could never have been brought about but for this astonishing man who· for thirty-five years was the intimate adviser upon every type of bold and impudent experiment in French music, and whom Ravel was delighted to call, " a clumsy but talented explorer." At first Satie was surprised by this gratitude,[1] which found expression not only in the dedication to the last of the *Poèmes de Stéphane Mallarmé*, but, more especially, in the harmony of *Un grand Sommeil Noir* and *Sainte*, and the melodic and rhythmical structure of *La Belle et la Bête*, that delightful fourth *Gymnopédie*.

Though, as a child, as he himself admits, Ravel was sensitive " to every kind of music," bit by bit his cultural development revealed preferences : Schumann first of all ; then Weber, Chopin and Liszt appealed to him without mutually prejudicing each other. The passage of time, fresh discoveries and new loves never made him faithless to his early favourites. But it is very interesting to notice that the composers who most obviously influenced his early writing were two " outsiders " he took it into his head to approach when he was sixteen. To quote his own words :

" My first compositions,[2] which are still unpublished, date from about 1893. I was in Pessard's harmony class at the time. Emmanuel Chabrier's influence can be seen in the *Sérénade grotesque* for piano ; Satie's in the *Ballade de la Reine morte d'aimer*."[3]

No doubt because it is of slightly later date and a failure in his opinion, Ravel does not mention here a song to words by Verlaine, *Un grand Sommeil noir*, the manuscript of which

[1]" Whenever I meet him he assures me he owes me so much. It suits me well enough." (Letter from Erik Satie to his brother Conrad, 1911.)
[2] Biographical sketch.
[3] I do not know if the manuscripts of these works have been preserved.

is dated the 6th August, 1895.[1]   In its implacable monotony, it is a curious, moving work, and, thirteen years later, it was to find an echo in the Prelude to *L'Heure Espagnole*, and in the bell in *Le Gibet*. The harmony, which at the beginning is vaguely reminiscent of some *Lamento* by Henri Duparc, is mainly inspired by Erik Satie's *Sarabandes* ; but it was already differentiated from these by the strict sense of form which controls the movement of the parts.

" In 1895," Ravel goes on,[2] " I wrote my first published works : the *Menuet antique* and the *Habañera* for piano. I consider that in embryo the latter work embodies many of the elements which were to dominate my later compositions, and which through Chabrier's influence (as for instance in the *Chanson pour Jeanne*) I have been able to crystallize."

The *Habañera* for two pianos (which will be found orchestrated but unmodified in the *Rapsodie espagnole*), is probably an example without parallel of a great artist who reveals his capacities in his first published piece of work.   This unforgettable work, the delight of every musician, with the exception of the man who wrote it, has the strength of a prophecy assured of its fulfilment.   Those who first heard it did not understand it, and the interplay of influences do not help to explain it. Those harsh, compact chords which emphasize the line of a caressing and fluent melody : the persistent, sustained internal pedal, against which the rhythm is shattered, and the brilliance of the harmonies brightened by the impact of an implacable C sharp, which at once sustains and clashes with them : those cadences whose unanticipated logic have the surprise of unexpected fulfilment ; this impassioned, yet sensitive music foreshadows and epitomizes all the fascination and power which Ravel was not to develop till much later, all the wizardries of an art which here appears in its first brilliance and the pristine freshness of its full array, the perfect insect emerging from the chrysalis.

The *Menuet antique* for piano, composed during the same year, 1895, is quite a different matter.   In its scintillating lightness of approach, it continues the conflict between academic rigidity

---

[1] The ms. of *Un grand Sommeil noir* belongs to M. Lucien Garban, who has very kindly let me see it.

[2] Biographical sketch.

and adventurous experiment. A piece whose very title is paradoxical, it sets out to resolve the old quarrel between order and adventure within the framework of a clearly-defined form. It is with the hand of a master that the pupil juggles with his formula. Academic elegance, accentuated by a trace of archaism, arises from the acid discords—secondary sevenths and ninths—a technique which is more skilfully handled in the *Sonatine* of 1905.

In the 1898 edition, I have seen an admirable dedication to the *Menuet antique*. With no lack of humour, Ravel offers " this somewhat retrograde work " to his old master, Henri Ghys.

CHAPTER III

WITHOUT MAKING FALSE MOVES AND AS THOUGH THROUGH A natural development, by his twentieth year Ravel had extracted the first and most important elements of his style from among a number of possible courses.   He was far from underestimating the effort involved :   study and practice, analysis and calculation developed, clarified and sharpened his critical faculty.   And this critical sense became so much the more sure and unhampered since it never attempted to force the creative instinct onward, that instinct which was illuminated without being forced, and guided as it were unseeingly.

Even at this stage, Ravel was wary of submitting the powers of art to the fluctuations of sentiment.   He read the *Philosophy of Composition*, and took over in its entirety Edgar Poe's diatribe against those fanatical subjectivists who try to " transform the undercurrent of the theme into the upper and visible one."

Those of his friends who were attending Massenet's lectures in composition, gleaned an aphorism from this ingenious and sensible master which so delighted him that he quoted it all his life :   " In order to know your own technique, you must learn the technique of other people."

He learnt the technique of the classics.   He made a methodical analysis of the scores of Liszt, Chopin and Chabrier.   The *Prelude à l'après-midi d'un Faune* enthralled him and revealed Debussy to him in the first glory of his genius.   Then he discovered Borodin and the Russian School.   But he had already found himself and so much the more surely in that he did not try too hard to be original.   As a result, his personality seemed the more striking, since the objectivity which separated him from his own work served also to distinguish him from the run of students about him.   Above all, his ironical reserve was sufficient indication that he meant to keep free of easy acquain-

tanceships.   One of his fellow-students, Alfred Cortot, who had
studied him closely, and understood him well, described Ravel
in the nineties as a " deliberately sarcastic, argumentative and
aloof young man, who used to read Mallarmé and visit Erik
Satie."

His literary interests, although not very wide, reached
fastidious depths and corresponded surprisingly with his
æsthetic views, which hardly were to vary any more than the
choice of his bedside books.   Baudelaire—the Baudelaire of the
Art romantique, Curiosités esthétiques and *Journaux intimes*, and
through Baudelaire, Edgar Poe—Edgar Poe of the *Philosophy of
Composition* and *The Poetic Principle*—were to be the prophets of
his creed, and Stéphane Mallarmé his favourite poet.   He was
heard to bestow extreme praise upon *l'Eve future* by Villiers de
l'Isle-Adam and J. K. Huysmans' *A Rebours* as novels of
sophistication and artificiality.   As for his philosophical reading, it fastened curiously on Condillac's *Traité des Sensations*
and Diderot's *Paradoxe du Comédien*.   In 1896, the setting of
Sainte was to show a double attraction towards the icy purity
of Mallarmé's poems and the esoteric harmonies of Satie.

Ravel joined André Gédalge's counterpoint class the following year.   The same year, he began studying with Gabriel
Fauré, who had just succeeded Massenet in the Chair of
Composition.   Like old Grétry, he firmly believed that " it's
only in the middle of the shop itself that you can make a
selection," and " you cannot be simple, expressive and, most
important of all, accurate, unless you have exhausted the
difficulties of counterpoint " ;   and so he gladly submitted to
the strenuous and forceful discipline which this remarkable
teacher imposed on him :   " I am glad to be able to say," he
wrote later on, [1] " that I owe to André Gédalge the most
valuable elements of my technique.   As for Fauré, his *artist's*
advice gave me encouragement of no less value."

Ravel himself causes me to emphasize this word, believing
as he did with all the gentle and loyal respect he felt for Fauré,
that as far as he was concerned, he owed less to the criticisms
of the professor than to the suggestions of the great artist.   It
is perfectly understandable.   Fauré's class was to musicians a
little like Mallarmé's salon to the poets :   a delightful place,

[1] Biographical sketch.

25

conducive to informal conversation, where the secrets of the art of music were suggested, and the laws of sensuous enjoyment propounded gently to the ear without being dogmatically forced upon the mind. The best musicians of the time, with few exceptions, passed through this important academy of elegance and taste. Maurice Ravel gained from it what he had come to take, and more ; but he could not always give that kind of satisfaction one might reasonably have expected from a pupil with a less strongly marked personality. The propensities he displayed there were not less respected because they were not always praised. Should proof be needed, it could be provided by a small instance which the pupil liked to recall much later on, illustrating the open-mindedness and loyalty of the master.

A composition exercise had been returned to Ravel with very strong criticisms. At the next lesson, Fauré asked him for the pieces which he had so severely criticized. " As you found them so detestable, I didn't like to refer to them again."— " I may have been wrong."

The music of Maurice Ravel first appeared before the critics and the public on the 5th March, 1898. Young composers had not then available the endless outlets which are nowadays open to campaigns of the avant-garde. The groups which split up and wrangle over the most varied æsthetic manifestations — even æstheticism — had yet to appear. The *Société Nationale de Musique*, that bastion of French nationalism, the official organ of the " Schola Cantorum," should, in justice bound, have tolerated all experiments, and accepted works quite foreign to its spirit. It is enough to note that the *Sites auriculaires*, if only because of its title, was excluded from the privilege of a favourable criticism.

The first of the pieces for two pianos collected under this *symboliste* description was none other than the amazing *Habañera* of 1895. The second, *Entre Cloches*, was more or less massacred. Marthe Dron and Ricardo Viñes, obviously hampered by a practically illegible manuscript, were so agitated that they struck chords together which should have been heard alternately. An attentive listener, whose memory may be trusted, remembers having distinguished in the hubbub combinations of chords in A flat " whose vibrations re-

echoing between the pianos sounded like the clash of brass.''[1]
Listeners less tolerant than Alfred Cortot, and a host of indignant critics, hailed the *Sites auriculaires* with ironical or outraged comments.

Such was Maurice Ravel's introduction to the public.

Towards the end of last century, young composers found it difficult to think of the theatre, let alone music, except in terms of Richard Wagner. Though by temperament and taste Ravel as a musician was remote from the Wagnerian technique and system of æsthetics, the reader of Villiers and Mallarmé was not able to ignore the fantastic element in the best pages of the *Ring* and *Parsifal*.

The German Romantics, Weber first and foremost ; Wagner at the height of his incantations ; the composers of the Russian School whose *Antar* and *Thamar* he had just heard ; they all withheld from him the golden keys of Faery, a kingdom which since childhood a secret but tyrannical impulse had made him long to enter. And this faery-land inspired his first attempts at drama, the first being the opera *Schéhérazade*, roughed out on a libretto which he selected himself from Galland's *Mille et une Nuits*, an episodic piece in which the characters were to revolve round the central figure of Schéhérazade.

The story-teller begins her tale in front of a heap of corpses of former sultanas. The back of the stage is then revealed to show Sindbad the Sailor's ship. After many vicissitudes, of which the last brings us back to the original scene, the Sultan, lost in his reverie, is loth to wake, and the hangman approaches Schéhérazade with the fatal rope in his hand.

This draft for a magic opera, in which the choruses and dances are closely bound up with the action, shows, even at this stage, the composer's desire to make the plot fit in with the symphonic demands. *Schéhérazade* was abandoned for *Olympia*, a fantastic tale inspired by Hoffmann's *L'Homme au sable*, in company with *Coppélia* and Offenbach's famous work.

From childhood Ravel was swayed by this strange passion for automata, an attraction not without a certain terror.

[1] Alfred Cortot : *La Musique française de piano*, Vol. II, page 26. *Entre Cloches* is still unpublished. Contrary to M. Cortot's conjecture, *La Vallée des Cloches* does not in any way hark back to it.

Before he could discover the secret of those steel hearts, or master their mechanical voices, this " Swiss clockmaker " brooded on their mysteries with a sympathy infinitely more solicitous and eager than his curiosity about human nature. Thus the symphony of clocks in *L'Heure Espagnole* started from the song of cylinders and springs which had accompanied the entry of the satanic Coppélius in the first scene of *Olympia*.

There only remains the Overture of *Schéhérazade*, conducted by the composer on the 27th May, 1899, at one of the orchestral concerts of the *Société Nationale*. It was hissed by the public and soundly rated by the critics :

" If that is M. Ravel's idea of an overture ' constructed on classical lines,' " wrote M. Pierre Lalo, " I must say that M. Ravel has a great deal of imagination. His structural approach reminds one of that of M. Grieg, and, even more of M. Rimsky-Korsakov or M. Balakirev. There is a similar incoherence in the general plan and in the tonal relationships ; but these characteristics, already sufficiently striking in the masters, have been carried to excess by the pupil . . . "

Ravel never allowed this overture to be published, but he used some of the material for a second *Schéhérazade*, a setting of poems by Tristan Klingsor. Part of it, in particular, provided the first theme for *Asie*. In later days, the composer's own opinion of this first attempt at symphonic writing " very strongly under the influence of Russian music "[1] was to exceed M. Lalo's criticism in severity. Ravel did not hesitate to confess that the overture was " badly constructed and crammed with whole-tone scales. There were so many of them in it, in fact, that I had enough of them for life."

A piano piece written in the same year—1899—which he criticized quite as harshly later on, was to experience an entirely different fate. The *Pavane pour une Infante Défunte*, which gained him the esteem of the salons and the admiration of young ladies who do not play the piano over-well, scarcely deserves, in the eyes of musicians, the extraordinary popularity which for thirty years it has enjoyed with the public at large. " I don't feel a bit embarrassed in talking about it," he wrote in February, 1912, in the *Bulletin de la S.I.M.* " It is so much a matter of ancient history that it is time the composer

[1] Biographical sketch.

handed it over to the critics. I no longer see its virtues from this distance. But, alas, its faults I can perceive only too well : the influence of Chabrier is much too glaring, and the structure rather poor. The remarkable interpretations of this inconclusive and conventional work have, I think, in great measure contributed to its success."

It is a stern verdict, but not an unjust one. The imitation of Chabrier—and Fauré as well—did not serve here to display his creative qualities, as it does elsewhere in Ravel's work. The writing and structure of this pavane is utterly unlike Ravel ; skilful orchestration has added a slightly monotonous charm and the very name has inspired girls, literary gentlemen and versifiers to send the composer their poetical or plastic interpretation of the *Pavane pour une Infante Défunte*. Ravel always replied : " When I put together the words which make up this title, my only thought was the pleasure of alliteration ..."

In 1901, candidates for the great *Prix de Rome* were asked to set—*secundum regulas artis*—a cantata by Fernand Beissier entitled *Myrrha*. A second prize was the reward Ravel had for his pains.

This devotee of Mallarmé, who was competing for the first time, does not seem to have been put out by the platitudes and absurdities of a text bristling with clichés and far surpassing in mediocrity the usual type of such hack-work :

> *Non ! je ne veux pas à cette heure*
> *T'arracher ici de mes bras*
> *Ici-bas il faut que je meure . . . etc.*[1]

clamours Myrrha at the most pathetic point in the great loveduet.

The pleasure Ravel always found in complying with the exigencies of a task whose rules had been formulated by a will counter to his own, finds a happy expression in the phrases of the slow waltz and the swooning melodies in which his cantata pretends to lose itself with a complacent skill not always very far removed from an ironic pastiche. Its success was great enough to make the adjudicators consider awarding him the first *grand prix* on the spot, a prize which he seems only to

[1] " Ah no ! not at this hour will I tear you from my arms. Here, here will I die," etc.

have lost by a hair's breadth. A letter to his friend, Lucien Garban, dated the 26th July, 1901, which he wrote " soothed by the twittering of the engines "[1] throws a humorous light on the undercurrent of academic debate :

" . . . Almost all the judges recommended me for the prize (Massenet voted this way in fact all along). I have been told something very curious : that I possess a spout of melody . . . . . from which there flows quite effortless music. This charming metaphor comes from your dear master Xavier Leroux, who, like Vidal, has shown himself very enthusiastic on my behalf. I have even been assured—*horresco referens*—that Lenepveu was very taken with my cantata, but not, mark you, quite enough to prefer it to that of his pupil.[2]

" ' Why didn't you get the first prize ? ' you will ask. Because, believe it or not, my orchestra played me a dirty trick. Although my composition was one of the first to be finished, I happened to arrive a little late, and had scant time for my orchestra which consequently was a trifle scamped.

" I'll have to begin again, that's all . . ."

The Conservatoire pupil who in this modest and bantering manner describes the background of this semi-triumph in the Schools, was the same Ravel who, at twenty-six, had just completed his *Jeux d'eau* on which there is set with bold vivacity the hallmark of mastery. For this slight work was to have profound consequences. From it there rapidly emerged a new piano technique, which made Ravel's contemporaries acknowledge themselves his debtors, however small their contribution to virtuosity.

Dieu fluvial riant de l'eau qui le chatouille.[3]

When he decided to translate and illustrate this line of Henri de Régnier's through the medium of his art, the composer of *Jeux d'eau* was not aiming to revolutionize piano-writing so much as to extend Liszt's experiments with the use of the high registers of the instrument in a fluent and sensitive manner whose vivacity was akin to the Sonatas of Scarlatti.

[1] The Ravel family had just settled at 19, Boulevard Pereire, after living in succession at 40, Rue des Martyrs, 29, Rue Laval, 71, Rue Pigalle and Rue Lagrange.
[2] André Caplet, who won the first prize.
[3] " A river-god laughing at the waters as they caress him."

According to his publisher Demets, Ravel was the first to be surprised by the sensation the work produced, and the influence it exercised upon the work of his contemporaries from the moment of publication. " So little did he believe in its success after he had written it," Demets acknowledged, " that after being compelled forcibly to wrest the manuscript away from him for printing, he persuaded me not to take out a copyright, with the result that a score of pirated versions of the French edition of *Jeux d'eau* exist in the U.S.A." Afterwards Ravel came to realize that *Jeux d'eau* was the starting-point for every pianistic innovation in his work which has since aroused comment.

" This piece, inspired by the sound of water and the music of fountains, waterfalls and streams, is built up on two themes like the first movement of a sonata, without being entirely subjected to the classical scheme of tonality."[1]

As for the influence of *Jeux d'eau* on the technique of his contemporaries, and especially on that of Debussy, he was bound to be convinced of it when he heard the pieces making up the collection of *Estampes*, written in 1903. He even needed to publish this evidence, in spite of his accustomed modesty and natural reserve, when a critic took it upon himself to praise Debussy for exactly the same methods exemplified earlier in Ravel :

" You dilate at some length," he wrote[2] to M. Pierre Lalo, on the 5th February, 1906, " upon a somewhat specialized kind of piano-writing, the invention of which you ascribe to Debussy. But *Jeux d'eau* appeared at the beginning of 1902, when the only works of Debussy in existence were the three pieces *Pour le piano*,[3] works which I need hardly say I passionately admire, but which, from a purely pianistic point of view conveyed nothing really new. I hope you will forgive this justifiable claim . . . "

It was indeed a strange period, when criticism, permeated by romantic subjectivism, required each artist to live in a world apart, and to develop not merely his own style, but a diction and vocabulary peculiar to himself ; a period when a

[1] Biographical sketch.

[2] Private letter published by M. Lalo in *Le Temps* on the 9th April, 1907.

[3] Ravel orchestrated its *Sarabande*.

classic craftsman who makes a principle of imitation, is blamed for yielding to forces which are precisely those he did *not* invoke, at a time when he was reproached for having been influenced by them !

CHAPTER IV

The "Apaches"—Ravel and Debussy—the Quartet in F—Schéhérazade—*the* Prix de Rome scandal—*the "Ravel scandal."*

LÉON-PAUL FARGUE CAME ACROSS A PHOTOGRAPH OF A GROUP taken in 1901 at the castle at Compiègne, during one of the leisure-periods allowed to candidates for the *Prix de Rome*. He describes Ravel as " wearing side-whiskers and a *cronstadt* hat, with his hand in his overcoat pocket, standing a little aloof from the other competitors, looking away from them. He had already ceased to look like the others ; he had lost that deceptive air of the gay and carefree student which distinguishes people who make a round of competitions . . . already his face showed some of the signs and shadows of the mature artist, resembling the harassed expression of a Baudelaire, or a Wagner ; he possessed as well their watchful, aloof dignity."[1]

This was the Ravel whom Léon-Paul Fargue met in 1902 at the house of Paul Sordes, that sensitive painter, ardent music-lover, reliable and tactful friend. Every Saturday Paul Sordes invited a small group of friends to his house in the Rue Dulong. The circle was open to all the changeable winds of fashion, but firmly closed to all pedants and spurious æsthetes : " We all read or played," said Fargue,[2] " whatever we had recently written or composed, in the most friendly atmosphere I have ever experienced." Regularity had never been Ravel's chief virtue, but he was always faithful to these reunions, which at the beginning included, apart from the host and his brother Charles Sordes, the poet Tristan Klingsor, the painters Edouard Benedictus and Séguy, Charles Guérin, Chanvin, and the musicologist M. - D. Calvocoressi, joined later by Maurice Delage (who became Ravel's pupil and his most intimate friend), D. E. Inghelbrecht, Lucien Garban, Marcel Chadeigne, Ricardo Viñes, the decorator Georges Mouveau, and the designer Pivet.

[1] Léon-Paul Fargue : *Maurice Ravel*, in *Plaisir de France*, August, 1936.
[2] Ibid.

At about one in the morning Fargue used to ring a bell to remind them that it was necessary to remember the neighbours and close the piano.

In 1904, the " assembly " removed to Maurice Delage's quarters, as he had just recently rented a summer-house at the bottom of a garden at Auteuil, in the Rue de Civry, " neat as a doll's house, a little masterpiece of a house with no neighbours, where we could make music all night long when we had missed the last train home."[1] There the group gathered new recruits : Joaquin Boceta, " a young Spaniard crazy about music and mathematics," Florent Schmitt, who had returned from Rome via the Caucasus, Austria and Germany, Déodat de Séverac, André Caplet, Paul Ladmirault ; Cipa Godebski, Synnesvedt, Manuel de Falla, Maurice Tabuteau, the future aviator, and the Abbé Léonce Petit, future chaplain of the Opéra—*in partibus infidelium*. This little company held its meetings regularly right up to 1909, when it admitted its last member—a young composer, Igor Stravinsky.

The circle often went to a concert or a performance of *Pelléas et Mélisande*. One evening, coming out from a function of this sort, Ricardo Viñes, who was leading the procession, was hustled along by a paper-seller, who pushed him out into the passage yelling hoarsely : " Look out for the ' Apaches,' " " They're calling us the ' Apaches ' now," said Viñes, and from then on the word served to describe the group.

The " Apaches " had code words to get rid of those who irritated them, and secret signs for finding each other. They would make an excuse to leave some bore by saying they had to meet a certain Gomez de Riquet. This Gomez de Riquet was an imaginary character invented by Ravel. The first theme of Borodin's Second Symphony, when softly whistled, acted as a rallying-call.

" We had more or less the same tastes in art," wrote Fargue, " which was lucky for people as hot-headed as we were, because, as someone has said, you can't discuss things except with people of your own opinion, and even then only questions of fine distinctions. Ravel shared our preference, weakness or mania respectively for Chinese art, Mallarmé and Verlaine, Rimbaud and Corbière, Cézanne and Van Gogh,

[1] Léon-Paul Fargue : op. cit.

Rameau and Chopin, Whistler and Valéry, the Russians and Debussy . . ."

The Ravel of side-whiskers and discreet but ceaseless concessions to the demands of fashion, presents the perfect type of Baudelairian dandy ; elegantly frigid, with a horror of triviality and all effusions of feeling. He had the proud reserve of a man with a message whose secret he had not as yet divulged. Thus the young man who went around with the "Apaches" seemed to be more frigid and self-contained to his youthful companions than the famous composer whom, twenty years later, so many people, at a loss for that type of cordiality which was not in him, were to praise for his courteous and smiling simplicity.

Already, music interested him less in its finished state than in the making. Long *séances* at the piano "between artists," were drudgery to him : "I've had enough of it as soon as I begin," he confessed to Maurice Delage. The "Apaches" of the Rue Dulong took it for granted, and hastened to make their music before he appeared.

In the heroic days of *Pelléas*, the "Apaches," as Debussy's champions, did not miss a single performance of his new masterpiece, and waged the battle in the front line, in other words, the topmost gallery ; even the Abbé Léonce Petit abandoned the breviary which he read in the intervals to join in the polite or impolite jousts enjoyed by the partisans and their enemies.

Ravel knew Debussy personally, and at the beginning their relationship was excellent. Although they were never intimate friends, they were at least good friends for a great many years. Because it gave him pleasure, and because he wished to pay homage to a man of genius, Ravel transcribed for two pianos the *Prélude à l'après-midi d'un Faune*, a work which he himself never tired of calling a masterpiece. "He knew and sincerely admired Debussy," wrote Louis Laloy in *La Musique Retrouvée*. "I did everything in my power to prevent a break between them, but too many stupid meddlers seemed to take pleasure in making it inevitable, by sacrificing, for example, Debussy's Quartet on the altar of Ravel's, or by raising absurd questions about the priority of the *Habañera* and the second of the *Estampes*. The two composers then stopped visiting each other ; and as their respect for each other was entirely mutual, I can vouch for the fact that they both regretted the rupture."

Not so much to invalidate the evidence of an accredited Debussyist, as to preserve a piece of enlightened commentary, I wrote down in 1912 the following utterance by the composer of the *Valses Nobles et Sentimentales* : " It's probably better for us, after all, to be on frigid terms for illogical reasons." All the same, the two composers kept up a social and artistic relationship up to 1902, at a time when Debussy's genius, which had arrived at maturity, was burning with its brightest flame and revealing its most engaging charm. Then, and only then, in Ravel's work could there be seen, in the String Quartet and the three *Schéhérazade* songs faint, but unmistakable, traces of Debussy's influence.

" My String Quartet," said Ravel,[1] "represents a conception of musical construction, imperfectly realized no doubt, but set out much more precisely than in my earlier compositions."

All the same, though not to contradict the composer, it is noticeable how, if this work really represents so absolute a conception of structure, it does so with extraordinary vigour, rhythmical ease and melodic verve. The intense suavity of this grave, youthful music makes it appear the most spontaneous work Ravel has ever written. The outbursts of lyricism find forceful expression within the framework of an uncompromising classicism without breaking it ; they move so freely within it that the composer sometimes used to doubt his success. The more the secret powers which governed him unawares attracted him, the more he mistrusted them. He was suspicious of the lure of spontaneity which had led him so easily from the arbitrary to the necessary, to borrow a happy phrase from Paul Valéry. Contrary to his practice, he submitted his work to the judgment of his friends, and the criticism of the master to whom it was dedicated. Fauré did not mince matters. He found the fourth movement stunted, badly balanced, in fact, a failure. In the end, Debussy was asked for his opinion, and he reassured and congratulated the younger man, writing him a solemn injunction : " In the name of the gods of music, and in mine, do not touch a single note of what you have written in your Quartet."

[1] Biographical sketch.

Debussy was obeyed.

The three *Schéhérazade* poems originated in the circle of the "Apaches." The charming and versatile Tristan Klingsor, not content with supremacy in painting and poetry, teased all the Muses, and came to no harm. At this particular time he had written some songs, and in 1903 published a book of poems—*Schéhérazade*. " Ravel immediately wanted to set some of them," wrote Klingsor : " his love of difficulty made him choose, together with *L'Indifférent* and *La Flûte Enchantée*, one whose long narrative made it appear quite unsuitable for his purpose : *Asie*. For at that time he was engaged in a study of spoken verse, and was aiming at emphasizing accents and inflections and magnifying them by melodic transposition ; to fix his design firmly, he insisted on my reading the lines aloud."

These three poems for voice and orchestra " where," declared Ravel,[1] " Debussy's spiritual influence at least is fairly obvious, date from 1903. In them, again, I have succumbed to the profound fascination which the East has held for me since childhood."

In *Schéhérazade*, first sung by Mme Hatto at the *Société Nationale* on the 17th May, 1904, under the direction of Alfred Cortot, Ravel did more than merely recast parts of the overture of the same name : by keeping to the images and words woven by the poet's fancy, the composer of *Asie* obeyed that formal preoccupation demanded by the earlier " færie," and made use of a similar device. The music keeps close to the narrator, leaves him and then returns in such a way as to " interrupt the tale artistically." The result is that this poem, much more developed than the other two, maintains a stylistic unity in its continuous diversity of episodes.

Apart from the personal idiom of the orchestral writing, the style of this evocation, the quality of its harmonies, and, above all, the charm of the declamation, convince me that Ravel was never closer to Debussy than at the beginning of this imaginary voyage. But already in the counterpoint of *La Flûte Enchantée* he goes his own way and still more in the dignified melody of *L'Indifférent* which resists the ambiguous and secret fascination of Klingsor's " musique fausse."

[1] Biographical sketch.

As Ravel's creative mastery grew more assured, he began to see his star pale in the academic firmament :

Alcyone ! Alcyone ! Aimée ! Aimée ! Hélas !

The 1902 Cantata in which, according to Calvocoressi, this sublime alexandrine was sung, was only to M. Aymé Kunc's advantage. *Alyssa*, written during the next year, was no more successful. Gabriel Fauré was roused to vigorous protest.

Ravel does not seem to have inordinately desired the sanction of the *Prix de Rome* ; but once he was launched on a venture, his nature compelled him to see it to a satisfactory conclusion. He nerved himself for the task, and all the more because he wanted his parents, to whom he was devoted, to have the satisfaction of a success afforded by official recognition. Apart from this, to be quite frank, his family were not rich, and the *Prix de Rome* ensured its recipients several years of financial security.

Although in 1904 he had given up the thought of competing, Ravel decided the next year to try his chance for the last time. At this point the judges of the preliminary competition made the amazing decision to exclude him from the final trial, thus preventing a candidate who had been successful four years earlier from competing. What had taken place in the interval ? Why was he to blame ? Was he no longer capable of writing fugues and choruses ? What sins, what crimes had he committed in those four years ?

Manifestly these crimes were *Jeux d'eau*, the Quartet, and *Schéhérazade*. They were so serious that their perpetrator could no longer plead ignorance of the precepts of that childish and well-meaning civility which he had so well, almost too well, observed, to please his teachers. So it was with full knowledge of the facts that he transcended and transgressed these precepts in the works he had been simple enough to publish in his own name. Far more than an error, it was an act of heresy, since he knew what ought to be done, and chose to do what he did. A judgement made some while before by a member of the Musical Section of the *Académie des Beaux-Arts* gave the final verdict : " M. Ravel may well take us for windbags ; but not with impunity will he take us for idiots . . . " So there !

Academic juries do not enjoy the privileges of anonymity as do juries on assize. So it is easy to nominate for public prosecution Charles Lenepveu, Théodore Dubois, Paladilhe, Massenet, and Reyer, members of the *Institut*, and the co-opted members Xavier Leroux, Hillemacher and Roujon. The music critics did not do badly. Jean Marnold, a vehement fighter, was the first to enter the lists, vested with authority by his article published in April, 1904, when he had prophesied events, and hailed the composer of the String Quartet as " one of the masters of the future." The impetuous critic of the *Mercure de France* was not at all half-hearted ; after commenting that the " outlaw benefited by Reyer's ostentatious support," Jean Marnold revealed that all the candidates approved were found to be pupils of the same Lenepveu who sat on the jury as he sat at meetings of the *Académie* " between MM. Paladilhe and Dubois, of course." And rather crudely the journalist goes on to ask if in future the *Prix de Rome* will be " wrested away by intrigue, or awarded by idiots."

The scandal passed beyond musical circles. The press outside echoed it. Alfred Edwards knew and admired Ravel. *Le Matin*, which he edited, took sides in the quarrel. There was a Ravel scandal, and all Paris society, except the victim himself, was stirred by it ; even M. Romain Rolland was involved, and although his musical taste did not agree with Ravel's inclinations, he generously protested against an iniquitous judgement.

The campaign could not repair the irreparable. It could not help Ravel, who neither complained nor asked for anything. None the less it had a fortunate result which was to benefit the official teaching of music ; for it seems likely to have brought about the resignation of Théodore Dubois, Director of the Conservatoire, and the nomination of Gabriel Fauré in his place.

CHAPTER V

ALTHOUGH RAVEL SEEMED UNCONCERNED AND UNAFFECTED BY misfortune and antagonism, he could not help being secretly affected. The friendship of Alfred Edwards and his wife, formerly Godebska, provided a pleasant diversion, the leisurely enjoyment of a yachting cruise in Holland, a country he had always wanted to know.

On the 2nd June, 1905, at the same time as Jean Marnold's philippic was appearing in the *Mercure de France*, Ravel was busy pursuing the river-yacht *L'Aimée* which he had missed ; he caught it up at Soissons where the owners of the boat and the artists Bonnard and Laprade were waiting for him.

On his return from this enjoyable trip, he was seized by a passion for work which, as his correspondence shows, surprised even him. What was admirable in this frenzy was that it did not die after its first flare-up ; without any effort a ceaseless variety of work was produced, none of which was negligible.

Ravel breathed again. He felt free of all academic obligations. He was released from show fugues and idiotic cantatas. His strong love of discipline—his greatest aid—did not prevent a feeling of relief. To be sure he already realized that no one ever finishes learning a technique, and that, after all, the aim of writing is only to write better ; but nobody could fail to agree that in this respect the Conservatoire, if not perhaps music itself, had nothing more to teach him.

A period of immense creative activity began for him. In three years, from 1905 to 1908, he was going to build up that part of his work which was not to be the least important or the least characteristic, since it was to contain the *Sonatine*, the *Miroirs*, the *Histoires Naturelles*, the *Rapsodie espagnole*, *L'Heure Espagnole*, *Gaspard de la Nuit*, *Ma mère l'Oye*, not to mention smaller works or the already well advanced sketch for *La Cloche engloutie*.

The Sonatine, written in 1905 for a competition organized by a musical review, was published at once by Durand, who soon became Ravel's accredited publisher.

For executants and the public at large, this tense and nostalgic composition has rapidly acquired a popularity infinitely more justifiable than that of the *Pavane pour une Infante Défunte*. The passionate surge of the first movement, the tender, nostalgic grace of the *Minuet* and the nervous vivacity of the *Finale* bear the double imprint of youth and mastery. The almost meridional brightness and clear outline of the *Sonatine*, the concise lyricism, the ingenuity of the melodic style, emphasized rather than hindered by the structural austerity, give it a classic character.

Form . . . .

One evening, after he had been giving his interpretation of *Un cahier d'esquisse* to the famous composer of this little-known work, Viñes arrived at the Rue de Civry still enraptured by what he had just heard : Debussy had told him that he hoped to compose music with a form so free as to seem like an improvisation ; and to write works which gave the impression of being taken straight out of a sketch book.

Ravel was there that evening. Contrary to expectation, he approved of the idea. He admitted that the work he had on hand was concerned with a similar problem : " I should like to do something to help me shake off *Jeux d'eau*." Shortly afterwards Ravel played *Oiseaux Tristes* to his friends.

" The *Miroirs*," said Ravel,[1] " are a collection of piano-pieces that mark a change in my harmonic development that is so profound that they have put many musicians out of countenance who up to that point have been the most familiar with my style.

" Chronologically the first of these pieces—and the most typical of them all—is, I think, the second of the group : *Oiseaux Tristes*. (In it I evoke) birds lost in the torpor of a sombre forest during the most torrid hours of summertime."

It is worth remembering Ravel's descriptive aim. It is an intention which will appear on every page of a collection whose very title is significant and a remarkable illustration of Ernest Hello's admirable aphorism : " The characteristic of

[1] Biographical sketch.

art is to suggest an as yet uncreated harmony by showing an image of it in a mirror."

In the *Miroirs*, though he may perhaps not have been aware of it, Ravel was harking back to a secular tradition of French music which, unlike Beethoven, preferred to " paint " rather than to " express emotion." He sought not so much to express and give life to states of mind as to represent the faces and scenes which gave rise to them. " If music can describe an object without first revealing the artist," as André Suarès has so well said, " then Ravel's music succeeds better than any one else's "—and the music of the *Miroirs* in particular.

These five pieces, in which, with assured freedom, Ravel makes use of a completely new style, show by their dedications that they are perfectly in keeping with the spirit of the " Apaches " : thus Léon Paul Fargue is presented with the *Noctuelles*, Ricardo Viñes the *Oiseaux Tristes*, Paul Sordes *Une Barque sur l'Océan*, Calvocoressi *L'Alborada del Gracioso* (Morning-song of the Jester), and Maurice Delage *La Vallée des Cloches*.

The *Miroirs* reveal a structure no less clear because it is pliant. The rhythmical solidity is broken up. The range of modulation is extended. The harmony, especially, is enriched daringly ; it is thrown into extraordinarily clear relief. It surpasses the expectations raised by the astonishing *Habañera* of 1895. Yet far from involving Ravel " in the pure, viewless delight " of sensation enjoyed and pursued for its own sake, this boldness brings him back again to the substantial realities of music and makes him cling more tenaciously than ever to the golden thread of tonality.

Difficult as they are to play, these pieces at first seem to be equally difficult to understand. Even Ravel's followers were divided for a long time over the " sincerity " of the *Oiseaux Tristes*. Even today pianists are intimidated rather than charmed by these magic mirrors, only keeping in their repertory the *Alborada del Gracioso*[1] where the dry and biting virtuosity is contrasted, Spanish-wise, with the swooning flow of the love-lorn melodic line which interrupts the angry buzzing of guitars. It is an altogether admirable piece of

---

[1] " Gracioso," a pleasant, facetious character in Spanish comedy.

work, and doubly successful in the brilliantly orchestrated version.

It was in the same year, 1905, that Ravel, attracted as always by the theatre—and the "færie" quality which he never entirely dissociated from it—discovered on a bookstall by the Seine the German dramatist Gerhardt Hauptmann's *La Cloche engloutie* in the good French translation by A.-F. Herold.

This is a work where the fantastic is grafted upon the everyday, and where myth creeps into the framework of modern life. It had already tempted one composer, Zœllner, and was later to catch the attention of another, Ottorino Respighi. Ravel, continually aware of the mysterious appeal of the tick-tack of automata and the hum of machines, was delighted to think he held the book of words which gave him the opportunity to introduce enchantment into the factory world.

Maurice Delage, who was beginning to be anxious at getting no answer to the letters and telegrams which he had sent to him one after the other, received a feverish letter from Ravel, written on 12th June, 1906, when he was closeted at Levallois[1] and completely absorbed in his great undertaking :

"For two weeks I haven't left the grindstone. I have never worked so ferociously. Oh yes, perhaps at Compiègne, but that was less fun. It's inspiring, writing a work for the theatre. I won't say that this came without effort, but it's certainly the best of the bunch. Ye gods ! in a few days I see my way clear. Anger, depression and bitter reproaches against my family for not having put me in a grocery shop. Never mind, there are some wonderful moments in this devilish work . . . "

On 20th August of the same year he was at Hermance on the Lake of Geneva, where he had accompanied his father who was beginning to suffer from the early attacks of an illness from which he died two years later. The place pleased Ravel, but not to the point of making him forget *La Cloche engloutie*. " . . . The colours are intense and paradoxical, the values false. And then, as well, there are the boats with

---

[1] After leaving the Boulevard Pereire, the Ravel family settled at Levallois-Perret, at No. 11, Rue Chevallier.

their bright sails. Most remarkable of all is the mild and surprisingly pure climate. My father feels revived and says his head is not quite so painful. Even the local inhabitants are curious. I left a cousin doing watchmaking whom I've now found out to be first violin at the Geneva theatre.[1]

" I am waiting for a piano to get back to *La Cloche* which momentarily has been interrupted. . . . You can already imagine a great part of the second act in addition to what you know of the first. (Are you anxious to have an opera in five acts ? You'll have it in a week !)

" Interrupted by a gentleman who died last year. Will let you know the details later on."

In spite of the enthusiasm which this shows him to have had for the work in hand, *La Cloche engloutie* was abandoned for other work, then resumed and definitely abandoned in 1914. But he took its elements and made free use of them in the second act of *L'Enfant et les Sortilèges*, which obviously owes the theme of the tree and the chorus of frogs to *La Cloche engloutie*.

" Jules Renard's direct and clear language and his profound and obscure poetry (in the *Histoires Naturelles*) haunted me for a very long time. The text itself demanded a particular kind of musical declamation from me, closely related to the inflexions of the French language. The first performance of the *Histoires Naturelles* at the *Société Nationale de Musique* provoked a veritable uproar, followed by lively polemics in the musical press[2] . . . "

In the winter of 1906, when Ravel undertook the composition of these five songs, he would have been very surprised if anyone had prophesied that they would add more to his reputation than a large-scale work, or that these *Histoires Naturelles*, which he had originally thought of as an experiment in declamation, should make it possible for him, in spite of himself, to assert the brilliance of his personality, and also to discover his supporters thanks to a public scandal.

Nowadays it is difficult to understand how this pleasant work, whose very humour has resolved itself into pure music, managed to have offended so strongly the ears and tastes of

[1] His first cousin, Alfred Perrin, son of Louise Ravel.
[2] Biographical sketch.

44

its first listeners. In its obvious audacity it takes liberties which have since been imitated and surpassed so airily that we have got used to them : an audacity which consists in granting all the honours of song to the most gently harmonious prose, and, indeed, the most prosaic imaginable. From it there emerges a strange system of declamation which reconciles the exigencies of melody with those of French prosody—a system entailing a bold elision of silent vowels, one whose sudden aridity stands out in relief above a mysterious and graceful accompaniment.

For in this work (by a contrast, to be amplified later on in *L'Heure Espagnole*) it is the piano which undertakes the task of evoking the tranquillity of the "silent countryside," lending its tones to the mysterious chorus of disembodied beings.

Full of that apprehensiveness shot with contempt which intelligent men usually adopt about their own subjects Jules Renard, like Fontanelle, asked what music could want of him, but did not get a satisfactory answer. Much has been made of two passages in his *Journal* in which the over-sensitive poet refers to the composer of his *Histoires Naturelles*. And a curious testimony it is, but it tells us more about Renard than Ravel and it is difficult to take it unreservedly :

" 19th October, 1906.—Thadée Natanson told me :

" A musician wants to set some of your *Histoires Naturelles*. He is a composer of advanced views and no little importance, for whom Debussy is already a back stager[1] .... What do you think of that ? "

" Nothing at all."

" It must affect you, surely ! "

" Not in the slightest."

" What are you going to tell him ? "

" Whatever you want : thank him from me."

" Don't you want him to let you hear his music ? "

" Oh ! no."

" 12th January, 1907.—M. Ravel, the composer of the *Histoires Naturelles*, dark, rich[2] and subtle, insists on my going

---

[1] Natanson freely attributes to Ravel an opinion he never held.

[2] Where the dickens had Renard got hold of the idea that Ravel was rich ?

to hear his songs this evening. I told him how little I knew about it, and asked him what he could add to the *Histoires Naturelles*."

" My plan isn't to add to them but to interpret them."

" But what's the connection ? "

" To say in music what you say in words. . . . There is one sort of music which is instinctive and sentimental, [?] like mine, though granted you first need to know your job ; and there is the other sort—intellectualized music like d'Indy's. Only d'Indy's supporters will be present tonight, and they do not admit to an emotion they have no wish to account for. [?] I hold the opposite viewpoint : but they find my work interesting. To me this is a very important test, and anyway I have no doubts about my wonderful interpreter."

This dialogue is full of improbabilities. It credits Ravel with opinions and expressions so entirely foreign to him that at least the authenticity of the declaration on " sentimental " music and the last sentences must be called in question— except the praise of the singer Jane Bathori, who was really first-class and most heroically faithful to her composer.

It was tempting the devil to propose to present the delicate mockery of the *Histoires Naturelles* to the austere musical devotees who made up the public of the *Société Nationale*. The idea that poetry could arise from prose and be given life through contrast scarcely dawned on the audience who crowded the Salle Erard on 12th January, 1907. And when some days later M. Pierre Lalo said of it that " few subjects were more alien to music," he did not realize that it was just because they *were* alien that Ravel sought to naturalize them. But though the *Histoires Naturelles* reminded M. Lalo of the café-concert, " the café-concert with ninths," the work infuriated Auguste Sérieyx and his friends resolved to resist " mercilessly " an æsthetic opposed at every turn to their own form of sentimentality.

The business would have gone no further had not one of the opposition, namely M. Pierre Lalo, complained that in the *Histoires Naturelles* he constantly heard " the unmistakable echo of Debussy's music." It was not a new assertion : but in this case it was very difficult to maintain. It was taken up vigorously. The debate grew more venomous, and quickly degenerated into open conflict, giving rise to a second " affaire Ravel " at which Ravel might well laugh, but which focussed attention on the music of the young master and gave him the chance to count up his defenders and friends, in the front line of whom Jean Marnold, Louis Laloy, G.-J. Aubry and M.-D. Calvocoressi were fighting vigorously.

The latter was able to bring the thing to a head in a study sufficiently objective and level-headed to attract attention :
" It is very curious to note that the most frequent reproach made against the most experimental artists is that of plagiarism. . . . M. Debussy has enthusiastic supporters whose admiration, legitimate enough but pushed to extremes, leads them to formulate the strangest panegyrics upon his art : the composer of *Pelléas* has ' invented ' from nothing a musical language and an exceptional style which he has made his own. . . . A style . . . is the duly formulated result of a whole array of scattered tendencies, distant in origin and slow in development : it is the product of time. . . . Nobody has ever thought of claiming that Weber, Schubert and Beethoven, all three contemporaries, copied each other, on the pretext that they used the same rhythms, chords or melodic phrasing. . . . What is more, it is still true that modern means of musical expression are extraordinarily rich in new forms. Every one of the new idioms implied by such a transformation is striking to the listener solely because it is unusual : he notices nothing else and tends to isolate it in his mind ; and so much so, that while such a listener hears a succession of perfect dominant-tonic chords, and never thinks of associating them with one musician rather than another, he thinks of M. Debussy when he hears a chord of the ninth or the slightest suspicion of a second[1] . . ."

As remote as ever from the conflicts which made him their object, Ravel seemed by his silence to protest that the future of his works did not interest him. He was no more grateful to his supporters than resentful of his opponents. It is an undisputed fact that when public opinion, that world ruler, busied itself with his diminutive person, he was far from being concerned with recrimination, and willingly put space between

[1] *Grande Revue :* 10th May, 1907.

himself and the world. While the critics storm about his music, he boards *L'Aimée*, which was moored at Valvins, as at the height of the first " Ravel affair," and in one month composes the *Rapsodie Espagnole*.

The *Histoires Naturelles* were an exercise in declamation ; the *Rapsodie Espagnole* was primarily an orchestral study. The three poems of *Schéhérazade* had already shown the knowledge and power of a magician of " færie " when combined with an orchestral poet : a light and varied orchestration whose crystal-clear sounds gave question and answer. But in the *Rapsodie Espagnole* there is shown for the first time that taut and subtle orchestration, exemplified in the transparency, vigour and clarity of its outlines ; that pervading dry and silky quality in the orchestral colouring which serves to distinguish Ravel. No orchestration had as yet managed to obtain such trenchant *tuttis*, or such delicate pianos. Ravel, that mathematician of the mysterious, now knew how to judge imponderable tone value by the most sensitive and accurate balances imaginable.

It was not chance which led Ravel to introduce the *Habañera* of 1895 without modification into his *Rapsodie*. It is so much more appropriate there that it seems to have given something of its spirit to the other sections of this fantasy in the Spanish manner. In the *Prélude à la Nuit*, the imitative *Malagueña* or the vehement final *Feria*, stereotyped Andalusian formulæ are boldly introduced into the subtle symphonic texture. " Elements which are more or less objective," writes Alberto Mantelli, " a realistic rhythmical cadence and a decisive Spanish melody, give a texture to the work, which is quite different from the exquisite ambiguities of Debussy."

The first performance of the *Rapsodie Espagnole*, which was given at the Châtelet on 28th March, 1908, gave Ravel a chance to appear before a wider public—the semi-popular, excitable audience of the Concerts Colonne. Although the work was a little beyond the capacity of Edouard Colonne, who was kindly but a little aged, the performance was more or less satisfactory. The work received a courteous welcome from the audience, which turned to enthusiasm at the end of the *Malagueña*, encored at a request from the upper gallery. This encore was followed by certain ironical murmurs from

48

the orchestra stalls. It was then that the thunderous voice of Florent Schmitt asked from the top of the gallery for a second encore " just once more, for the gentlemen below who haven't been able to understand."

CHAPTER VI

L'Heure Espagnole—Ma Mère l'Oye—Gaspard de la Nuit—*death of Ravel's father*
—*Russian Ballet and the origin of* Daphnis et Chloé

WHEN " L'HEURE ESPAGNOLE " WAS FIRST PRODUCED AT THE Odéon, nobody could have known that Franc-Nohain's light comedy would become famous as an *opéra-bouffe*. Indeed, the charming Claude Terrasse, acting as a kindly intermediary, one lovely evening in 1906, between the composer of the *Miroirs* and the fanciful humorist of the *Poèmes amorphes*, was hard put to it to explain to the latter how a composer of serious and intellectual music could adapt himself to Franc-Nohain's derisive lyricism and sly mockery and to the complicated rhythm of his irregular metres and assonance, to say nothing of the licentious flavour of some of the scenes in the comedy.

At this period Ravel had not yet written the *Histoires Naturelles*, and besides *La Cloche engloutie* rumour had it that he was busy setting Maeterlinck's *Intérieur*—with which he did indeed toy for many years. In any case, no one imagined that he could be party to this free-and-easy farce, with its psychologically elementary intrigue, external complications peculiar to the sort of comedy which is dependent on words and situations, and contorted epigrams which seem to challenge music even more than the witticisms in the *Histoires Naturelles*.

All the same, the triumph of irony over poetry and the caustic tone of the comedy so defied the warmth of sensibility as to make Ravel feel drawn to try his luck. The atmosphere and setting also appealed to him as they were both favourite ones of his. The scene is laid in Toledo at a watch-maker's house ; thus under cover of an imaginary and fantastic Spain, the musician could call up the secret life of the pendulum, and the spirits of the chimes—all the clandestine life beating in the heart of the clocks. To cap everything, the ingenious drollery of metres and rhymes necessitated bold experiments in the tradition of *bouffe* recitative.

" The *Histoires Naturelles*," Ravel says, " paved the way for
L'Heure Espagnole . . . which in itself is a sort of musical
conversation. It reaffirms my intention to continue in the
tradition of *opéra bouffe*."[1] A conversation in music : that is
what *L'Heure Espagnole* is. But the success of this curious
masterpiece far exceeded its composer's expectations.

Ravel did not turn to account either the equivocal plot
of the farce or the vicissitudes which lead up to the statement
of the " moral," a moral which is taken from Boccaccio :

> *Entre tous les amants, seul amant efficace,*
> *Il arrive un moment dans les déduits d'amour*
> *Où le muletier a son tour.*[2]

He leaves to Franc-Nohain the tone of apparent artlessness
which makes the spectator blame himself for giving double
meanings to certain conversations which their author did not
intend to be perfectly innocent. Ravel did even more than
refuse to connive : instead of humanizing the characters, and
softening the passions which inflamed them, he ruthlessly
lays bare the elementary mechanisms of their instincts.
A casuist and surgeon, he uncompromisingly cuts out the
guileless or lascivious attraction each one possesses, and then,
by grafting a cylinder in place of a heart, changes them into
marionettes with cunning but frozen reflexes. But, by a weird
substitution, the hearts he tore from them come to beat
tenderly in the breasts of clocks and automata, lending to
these little steel bodies the semblance of a soul and the sweet
warmth of life.

L'Heure Espagnole was written without a break from May
to September, 1907, at Levallois, in the Rue Chevallier.
But the light-heartedness which dominated its creation, and
which the music reflects with so much brilliance, was
accompanied by secret haste and anxiety : Joseph Ravel
was growing old and his illness was becoming more serious
every day. The composer was more impatient than ever
to give his father, his incomparable father, one of those

[1] Biographical sketch.
[2]   Among all lovers the only effective lover,
            There comes a moment in the labyrinth of love
            When the mule-driver has his turn.

successes which only the theatre can confer, which seem like a seal set on good fortune. So he attempted to outpace the illness. Unfortunately he counted without his adversary.

Once the score had been completed, it had to be played over to the librettist. The piano-transcription and the composer's inadequate speaking voice always called for the use of the audience's imagination to make up for what could not be heard . . . Franc-Nohain had no musical imagination. The last chord of *L'Heure Espagnole* died away in silence. Thereupon the author of *Poèmes amorphes* brought out his watch and quietly muttered : " Fifty-six minutes."

A little later on the work was sent to the Director of the Opéra-Comique. M. Albert Carré was quite willing to accept it, but did not seem very anxious to stage it. Various considerations combined to defer the production of a work which was in every respect a difficult one. Not the least of the difficulties was the alleged " obscenity " of the libretto, a very formidable obstacle in a theatre frequented, at this time, by " respectable " engaged couples. M. Carré played for time, and season after season postponed the troublesome task of rehearsing *L'Heure Espagnole*. Nevertheless, it was produced in 1911, in circumstances to which I shall refer later.

" *Ma Mère l'Oye* (Mother Goose), juvenile piano-duets, dates from 1908. The idea of conjuring up the poetry of childhood in these pieces has naturally led me to simplify my style and clarify my writing. I have made a ballet of the work which has been put on at the Théâtre des Arts. The work was written at Valvins for my young friends Mimie and Jean Godebski."[1]

Ida and Cipa Godebski, the children's parents, had long been, and were to remain, staunch friends of Ravel, Fargue, Viñes, Maurice Delage—and all the little circle of the Rue de Civry.

After the group had broken up, most of the " Apaches " used still to meet on Sunday at the Godebskis' house in the Rue d'Athènes. There, in warm and discreet friendliness they met the group of writers who, along with Léon-Paul Fargue, were to contribute to the founding of the *Nouvelle Revue Française*.

Ma Mère l'Oye is an exquisite triumph. Because of its

[1] Biographical sketch.

atmosphere of happiness, tender emotion, and refined poetry, it is a work whose charm and popularity are the result of a supreme simplicity which never leaves it for one moment.

Fully in possession of himself and at the height of his powers, this ingenious craftsman momentarily stepped aside from the artificial beauty he loved to create. He knew, moreover, that simplicity can only be grasped effectively by means of the complex ; by elucidating and exhausting technical difficulties, Ravel undertook that clarification of structure and purge of texture, which, after the war, was to attract the best composers of the next generation as it did him ; but they sometimes ascribed too freely to Satie what in fact they owed to the composer of *Ma Mère l'Oye*.

Ravel was never more at his ease than in the children's kingdom of Charles Perrault, Mme d'Aulnoy and Leprince de Beaumont. By virtue of a privilege which he shared with the greatest creative artists, the composer never lost, in his obstinate determination to acquire technical mastery, that fresh sensibility which is the privilege of childhood and is normally lost with advancing years. He retained intact that freedom of imagination and artless power which in the adult generally gives way to the tyranny of fundamental instincts. Having arrived at that time of life when the capacities of youth delight in exercise, when power and knowledge become a joy, the Ravel of *Ma Mère l'Oye* shows us the secret of his profound nature and the soul of a child who has never left fairyland, who does not distinguish between the natural and the artificial, and who appears to believe that everything can be imagined and made real in the material world, if everything is infallibly logical in the mind.

To turn from *Ma Mère l'Oye* to *Gaspard de la Nuit*, composed at Levallois during the summer of the same year, 1908—is not to forsake the world of the fantastic but to find a changed climate. The clear and penetrating Ravelian melody which is emphasized by the two-part counterpoint in the *Pavane de la Belle au Bois Dormant*, or the parallel thirds in the *Petit Poucet* pastorale, demand, in *Ondine*, *Gibet* and *Scarbo*, a complex network of arabesques, muted, broadly-spaced chords, and dizzy flights in seconds. Perrault's place has been taken by Aloysius Bertrand, white magic by black.

Ravel already had a liking for romantic subjects which were to attract him progressively more. His treatment of them is far better when it is objective. He thought of romanticism as an animal to be tamed. The only thing to do is to keep out of the way of its attacks, and order it now to cringe and now to roar, a matter of courage and virtuosity.

Here, as elsewhere, Ravel in principle had simply aimed at the solution of a technical problem. As he said to Delage : " to write piano pieces of transcendental virtuosity which are even more complicated than *Islamey*." Transcendant : the word must be interpreted strictly since here virtuosity transcends its medium and turns *Gaspard de la Nuit* into one of Ravel's most personal successes, one of the peaks of his art. In it, all his qualities as a musician, and all the strength of his genius are crystallized ; particularly in the balanced richness and purity of melodic invention. For melody rules supreme. It gushes from the flood of arabesques, becomes silhouetted against them and mingles with them, only to stand out more clearly. In *Ondine* it touches the water-drops, in successions of light broken chords. In *Gibet* it is heard through the tragic knell of an internal pedal point, thus reviving and amplifying the enchantments of the *Habañera*. It turns about, is shattered, and finally is unified in the devilish scherzo *Scarbo*.

Never before had Ravel made such extensive use of the fascination of dreams, or the pervading enchantments of nocturnal visions ; artificiality had never so effortlessly or forcefully enhanced the semblance of the normal and the inevitable. Alfred Cortot accurately estimated the importance of the experiment. He considered that in *Gaspard de la Nuit* "the precision of a musical interpretation only makes the romantic exaltation of the literary argument more pronounced. . . . These three poems," continues M. Cortot, " enrich the repertory of our time by one of the most astonishing examples of instrumental ingenuity ever contrived by the industry of composers."

The death of his father, which took place on 13th October, 1908, darkened for him the end of a year which had begun so happily. His ardour for work was chilled forthwith.

Maurice Ravel belonged to that somewhat rare species of

spoilt children whose parents' affection has made them both imperious and passionately grateful. His feeling for them was compounded of silent adoration which he hardly ever showed to the outside world. Thus the only refuge and source of consolation for his troubles were solitude and silence.

1909 would have stimulated Ravel to nothing more than a little occasional piece, the *Menuet sur le nom d'Haydn,* had not the Russian Ballet suddenly appeared in the first flush of novelty to revolutionize the artistic world and urge a new direction on the activities of artists. The frenzied dancing, the sensuality of the music, the shock of the crudely coloured *décors* rivalled each other's audacity in dazzling confusion. A disturbing beauty emerged. The magic voice of the East was heard above the chorus of Sirens. Nowadays we accuse ourselves of having lent them too ready an ear. But it is far from true that all their counsels were as damaging to our art as has been made out. Every detail of the exotic ensemble was jealously planned in keeping with its essential spirit. Thus the Wagnerian fusion of the arts was followed by their conflict, the prelude to their separation. The Russian Ballet offered a battlefield to music and the plastic arts, in which each could arm against the others, and vie with each other's daring in glittering competition. Over and above all this, while the music of the " Five " was spreading the fame of the Russian School in France, and Bakst, Rœrich and Benois were reviving the art of *décor*, the choreographer Michel Fokine and the *maître de ballet* Cecchetti were restoring a tradition of dancing in France which rightly belonged to her, and was no less attractive now that it was disciplined by fifty years' exile in St Petersburg and Moscow.

During his production of the *Pavillon d'Armide, Les Sylphides, Cléopâtre* and the Polovtsian Dances from *Prince Igor*, Serge de Diaghilev was already fired by the inexorable passion for change, and planned to modernize his presentation. He made enquiries about new composers. Maurice Ravel was one of the first whom he sounded. He engaged him, introduced him to his last recruit, the young Igor Stravinsky, and put him in touch with Fokine, the choreographer of the troupe. Fokine described to Ravel his idea for *Daphnis et Chloé.* Ravel wanted nothing better than to write a ballet for the Russians, but he thought Fokine's plot feeble and unpleasing. He was given a rough copy, requested and obtained permission to modify it himself, and set to work rather reluctantly.

By March, 1910, the score was hardly begun. He retired to Valvins, to a villa owned by his friends the Godebskis, just near Mallarmé's country house. There he was overtaken by the floods. The water penetrated the ground floor of the house, but he did not bother about such a trifle. M.-D. Calvocoressi and Nouvelle, Diaghilev's colleagues, coming on a surprise visit, found him at the piano in a room whose floor was bending and swelling dangerously from the pressure of water.

He had resumed work on his first sketch, whose progress is curiously visible in the finished work. No ballet music was ever revised more successfully or polished with greater care. The *bacchanale* at the end, whose impetuous rush seems to be so convincingly effortless, cost its creator no less than a year of work. In the joy of perfecting his great choreographic symphony, the composer lost sight of the mediocre reason which had originally fired his imagination. But all the same, the inadequacy of this pretext was to appear in the performance of the work.

" I was commissioned by the Director of the Russian Ballet to write *Daphnis et Chloé*, a choreographic symphony in three movements. My aim in writing it was to compose a vast musical fresco, and to be not so much careful about archaic details as loyal to my visionary Greece, which is fairly closely related to the Greece imagined and depicted by French painters at the end of the eighteenth century.

" The work is constructed like a symphony, with a very strict system of tonality, formed out of a small number of themes whose development assures homogeneity to the work.

" *Daphnis et Chloé*, drafted in 1907 (*sic*), was several times revised, especially its finale." [1]

When Serge de Diaghilev entrusted *Daphnis* to the painter Léon Bakst and the music to Maurice Ravel, it did not occur to him to stipulate that artists so jealous of the autonomy

[1] Biographical sketch : Ravel is out by two years. The inaccuracy is obvious, as the first Russian Ballets date from 1909. I have stupidly reproduced the date in my earlier studies on Ravel, and the mistake has been copied by most other commentators who have wanted to make use of my facts.

of their respective arts should respect the primacy of dancing in ballet. As for Ravel, when he finished the score of his " choreographic symphony," he implicitly refused to humiliate himself before the feet of his dancers and claimed his right to dictate the law to them. Faithful to this claim in every respect it was inevitable that *Daphnis et Chloé* should burst its bounds, as of course it did.

Nevertheless, by virtue of its range, *Daphnis* remains the most important of Ravel's works. It may not appear from every point of view the most perfect—still less the boldest—and in some places it is even tainted with a suspicion of academicism, but all the same it contains some of the most effective and certainly the most warm-hearted music he has ever written. Its magnificence, and the sort of sublimity which is " controlled strength," are felt more obviously here than in his other works, among which *Daphnis* is remarkable for its astonishing sense of freedom. This freedom, this supreme lyricism are usually incompatible with an over-eager investigation into the sphere of the rare and original. So in this work one may expect to find less originality in the elements than power in the way they are fused. Whatever vague Debussyisms remain in *Schéhérazade* or the Quartet have vanished for ever. Melody is amplified and extended. The whole conception of the work is remarkable for its incomparable strength and ease. Its unified tonality is supremely successful.

This new leaning towards fresco and a style of greater scope and richness could not but influence the orchestration. The delicate graduation of colour and the taste for pure tones sometimes give way before the demands of symmetry and the necessity of thickening the texture.

Time and scene suggested the use of old tonalities. In addition, Ravel was naturally inclined to modes. So he did not have to modify his style to portray a Hellas which nevertheless takes little account of the text-books. If there is any archaism in *Daphnis et Chloé*, it is quite involuntary. I have quoted Ravel's confession that he was less consciously inspired by Mycenæ, Ægina and Byzantium than by the French painters of the Revolution. In passing, it is worth noting how his conception of the subject contrasts with that of the designer Léon Bakst.

57

CHAPTER VII

Foundation of the S.M.I.—the Valses Nobles et Sentimentales—L'Heure Espagnole
*at the Opéra-Comique—a trio of ballets—*Ma Mère l'Oye—Adélaïde—*first performances
of* Daphnis et Chloé.

IN THE SPRING OF 1910, A GROUP OF COMPOSERS, MOST OF THEM
pupils of Gabriel Fauré, decided to set up a new *pléiade*
in opposition to the *Société Nationale de Musique*, where a neo-
Beethovenian and Franckist system expounded by the doctrinaires
of the *Schola Cantorum* still reigned supreme ; their views were
to be more liberal, if not more coherent, and the presidency
was offered to the composer of *La Bonne Chanson.*

Ravel was one of the founders of the *Société Musicale Indépendante,* and reserved for it the first performances of his chamber
works. Thus *Ma Mère l'Oye* (Mother Goose) appeared on the
programme of the inaugural meeting of the S.M.I. on the
20th April, 1910, and the year following, on the 16th January,
the composer of *Gaspard de la Nuit* made a point of taking part in
a concert by the same society, dedicated to the works of Erik
Satie. In this concert he played the second *Sarabande,* the
third *Gymnopédie,* a prelude from the *Fils des Etoiles,* and, with
Ricardo Viñes, the *Morceaux en forme de Poire.*

The *Valses Nobles et Sentimentales* had just been completed
when the Committee of the S.M.I. decided, also during 1911,
to give a concert in which various works should be introduced
to the public without any indication as to their authorship.

" The title, *Valses Nobles et Sentimentales,*" said Ravel, " sufficiently indicates that I was intent on writing a set of Schubertian
waltzes. The virtuosity which formed the chief part of
Gaspard de la Nuit has been replaced by writing of obviously
greater clarity which has strengthened the harmony and
sharpened the contrasts . . . The *Valses* were first performed
to the accompaniment of hoots and cat-calls, at the concert of
the S.M.I., where the music was all anonymous. The audience
voted for the authorship of each piece. By a minute majority,
the paternity of the *Valses* was ascribed to me . . . . "[1]

[1] Biographical sketch.

First page of the manuscript *Valses nobles et sentimentales*.
Reproduced by kind permission of Messrs. Durand.

The identity of the composers had been kept so secret that not even the members of the Committee had known except where it was unavoidable. As for the *Valses*, only Louis Aubert was in the secret. As the interpreter of the work at this memorable concert, it was dedicated to him in recognition of his talent as a pianist as well as his discretion as a colleague.

The fact is that the public, mostly made up of professional musicians—and critics—appeared singularly nonplussed by the *Valses Nobles et Sentimentales*. So many votes wandered in unexpected directions : Zoltán Kodály, and Erik Satie, for instance[1] . . . Such howlers are surprising. But they·are explained by the peculiar audacity of a work which, to a marked degree, bears the imprint of its author, but which, by the very brilliance of its originality, could blind the music-lovers of 1911.

For the *Valses* hold a unique place in Ravel's work. It is quite easy to find pages which, on a first hearing, are more brilliant and easy to grasp ; but one cannot discover a work in which the material is more condensed, or where the form is more penetrating, elliptical and closely woven.

The one time Ravel condescended to express the secret of his inspiration by an aphorism, he came to the conclusion that his pieces had no motive beyond the " delicious and ageless pleasure of a useless occupation." [2]

Conditioned by this invocation of gratuitous enjoyment, the *Valses Nobles et Sentimentales* by their title acknowledge the patronage of Schubert, who, in his *Valses Nobles* and his *Valses Sentimentales*, intended to offer the " fair Viennese " the homage of a smile. A most engaging smile, too ; Chopin, before Fauré and Ravel, had not failed to succumb to it. This work of Ravel's forms a series of seven waltzes, each displaying a different demeanour despite their similarity of temperament, with a concluding epilogue in which the principal themes mingling with nostalgic grace, are re-echoed and gradually die away. Unconcerned with virtuosity, they do not pursue the path previously opened up by the *Miroirs* and *Gaspard de la Nuit*. Devoted to purely aural pleasure, they

---

[1] Alfred Cortot has insisted that I add the name of Théodore Dubois to the list, suggested probably by a voter who liked his little joke.
[2] This aphorism is borrowed from Henri de Régnier : preface to the *Rencontres de Monsieur de Bréot* (1904).

make the pianist's fingers oblivious of anything disquieting to the eye : numerous accidentals, lavished by a clever crafts-man, justify lively feats of daring and give them a rational basis.

It might be said that the composer profits by escaping from the tyranny of a set proposition and an exacting form in order to impose on his style a yet more stringent technique. How may he further lighten, without over-impoverishment, so tenuous a theme ? How sharpen still further its features without breaking the contour altogether ? In the *Valses Nobles et Sentimentales* problems such as these are solved with keen zest, as though they were child's play.

The harmony is shorn of the shimmer and glitter of doubled chords. The harmony grows dryer as it becomes clearer, increasing that transparency which emphasizes dissonance. Not content with eliminating the superfluous, the harmony goes so far as to give the impression of doing without the essential when it momentarily rejects the support of " good " intervals, and when it contrives loopholes in its texture to allow for the full development of a melody, continually re-newed as it comes in contact with steely counterpoint and chords of flint. In these waltzes Ravel is forced to give up his preference for the " grace-note " (or *note à côté*), imputed to him by harsh critics who have not studied Domenico Scarlatti, and who ingenuously give this name to the time-honoured practice of the acciaccatura. . . . A rather dry sensuality pervades the music—electric shivers and feline suppleness ; these, and the sort of evil fate which pursues them—typical Baudelairean delights.

Constantly spurned by pianists, the *Valses Nobles et Senti-mentales* suffer from warfare waged by that very snobbery they themselves mock. Orchestrated in circumstances to which I shall refer later on, their popularity is continually sacrificed to their younger sister, *La Valse*, which in no way equals them. Even though their name was changed for the purposes of ballet, they will not easily escape this fate.

The score of *L'Heure Espagnole*, published by Durand in 1910, was still waiting for the attention of the Opéra-Comique. This long-awaited production made Gaston Carraud say that M. Ravel enjoyed the same privileges as Richard Wagner . . At last, in 1911, after the good offices of a magnanimous lady, Mme Jean Cruppi, who was also an excellent musician, M. Albert Carré decided to start rehearsing the work.

L'Heure Espagnole was carefully produced. One of the best of the French theatre conductors, M. François Ruhlmann, made excellent use of the orchestral rehearsals, and the casting was good. Mlle Geneviève Vix, in particular, was given the finest opportunity of displaying her qualities as musician and comedienne in the difficult rôle of Concepcion. The other characters were very well played by MM. Coulomb (Gonzalve), Delvoye (Don Inigo), Cazeneuve (Torquemada) and by the great lyric comedian Jean Périer, who gave a notable performance as Ramiro, not his usual type of rôle.

L'Heure Espagnole was first performed on the 19th May, 1911, together with Massenet's *Thérèse*, not his best work. The audience gave it a courteous reception. Press opinion, taken all in all, was less favourable :

" *L'Heure Espagnole* is a curious and singular work," wrote M. Pierre Lalo, "without any doubt the most obviously successful that M. Maurice Ravel has produced, and one in which the personality of this young musician is most clearly revealed . . . His comedy, precious, dry and stiff, never relaxes or seems free for one moment. His characters in the highest degree lack life and soul. . . . Even the declamation which M. Ravel gives them . . . declamation reminiscent of that in *Pelléas*, played on a gramophone record at an excessively reduced speed, increases their resemblance to talking and singing automata. Everything about them is frozen and icy ; and everything is small, petty, narrow and attenuated : their height, carriage, gestures, even their talk and accent . . . This impression of something inanimate, artificial, mechanical and frozen . . . is lessened in actual performance because of the orchestration. The orchestral writing of *L'Heure Espagnole* is charming, striking, individualistic, varied, full of subtle timbres and rare combinations of sounds ; up to now the most attractive orchestration produced by M. Maurice Ravel . . .

" M. Ravel is entirely under Debussy's influence in passages of descriptive music, for, having no sensibility of his own, he borrows not only the technical apparatus but even the sensibility of someone else. But in a work like *L'Heure Espagnole*, from which all sentiment is banished, M. Ravel's original nature is apparent, and his ingenious and subtle insensibility gives it a personality of its own." (*Le Temps*, 28th May, 1911).

M. Emile Vuillermoz doubts the wisdom of the *quasi-parlando* recitative in *L'Heure Espagnole* : " In the name of logic Ravel removes from the language of music not only its internationalism and universality, but also its simple humanity . . ." Nevertheless, the symphony of clocks disarmed the severity of the chief editor of the S.I.M. Review : " What does this painstaking renovation of the accepted style of comic opera matter, if, as a result, we are given a page of pure music, such as that which accompanies the ' chorus of little voices ' from the watchmaker's shop, a prelude whence harmoniously exhales the singing soul of everyday things, where one hears, exalted and multiplied, all the secret, distant poetry of minute steel organisms, which the ingenuity of a craftsman has enriched with shrill, supernatural voices." (S.I.M., 15th June, 1911.)

With accurate feeling for Ravel's art, M. Henri Ghéon wrote a critical estimate in the *Nouvelle Revue Française* which was altogether favourable to the work, with the exception of one comment, which is highly valuable as it suggests the exact line of development which later on proved to be the one Ravel followed :

" The music of M. Ravel is, as regards its style and its tenets, French. His special and inborn talent—which he cultivates— is to translate into music the most unmusical subjects . . . It is miraculous to see how M. Franc-Nohain's buffoonery, whose comedy lies in gestures rather than in words, becomes the jumping-off ground for those unexpected but unrestricted arabesques, based on the spoken word but melodic all the same ; to see how an art, so concentrated and absorbed by the problems of expression, can give the impression of being so natural. His grace and gaiety, in my opinion, are supremely vocal ; in spite of the intellectual labour expended in the harmonic substance and the combinations of sound, I consider that the orchestra is given too much prominence in this work, that it is too noisy, that here was an opportunity to rebel against the use of orchestral masses with which, since Wagner, we have been overburdened . . . The way lies open for M. Maurice Ravel . . . to lighten music materially just as he has already done spiritually." (N.R.F., 1st July, 1911.)

On the evening of the first performance, the composer of *L'Heure Espagnole* saw Maurice Delage rushing towards him with a face in which shame and emotion were struggling for mastery : " Have you noticed," said Ravel to him without further preamble, " how you and I are the only people who are still wearing black evening dress ? You can't possibly fail to have noticed that nowadays ' everybody ' has succumbed to the fashion of the blue tails . . . Of course, its dark blue, which looks black in the light . . . "

The annual closing of the Opéra-Comique interrupted the performances of *L'Heure Espagnole*. Fate which, all considered, proved unkind, willed that it was never to open again at this theatre. The abandonment of the work resulted in persuading the Director of the *Académie Nationale de Musique*, M. Jacques Rouché, to make a fresh production of the unacknowledged masterpiece, shortly after the war. Contrary to all expectations, and in spite of its dimensions and the kind of work it was, it appeared more advantageously in the enormous Opéra than on the tiny stage of the Rue Favart. Clever staging, an ingenious *décor* by André Mare, which, by juggling with perspective, made it appear like a picture, and a first-class vocal interpretation (a triumph for Mlle Fanny Heldy) gave the work such a favourable hearing that this second production was instantly and unquestioningly acclaimed. It was the most brilliant new item in the Opéra's repertory. The success of *L'Heure Espagnole* spread even more quickly in the provinces and abroad. New York, Chicago, Brussels, London, Vienna, Berlin, Prague, Buenos Ayres : fifty cities were loud in praise of *L'Heure Espagnole*.

After *L'Heure Espagnole*, Ravel's music was in demand everywhere. Although no one could manage to wrest *Daphnis et Chloé* from the composer, as he was constantly revising and retouching it, he was persuaded to adapt to the exigencies of the theatre at any rate those of his works which would lend themselves to possible transformation.

For Ravel, it was a game, a game played to perfection, this metamorphosis of piano-pieces into symphonic works, so that the transcriptions outdid the charm of the original versions. This ability, misjudged by pianists, reached its highest pitch in the *Tombeau de Couperin*. *Ma Mère l'Oye* and the *Valses* had

Maurice Ravel in 1908 (Lucien Garban).

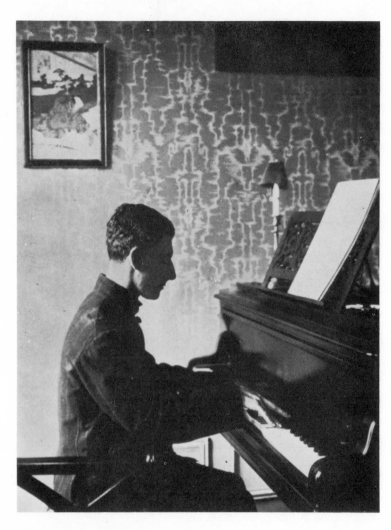

Ravel at the piano in 1912 (Roland-Manuel).

long before been given up to the demands of orchestra and choreographer.

1912 for Ravel was a year of ballets.

M. Jacques Rouché did not wait for the abandonment of *L'Heure Espagnole* before evincing sympathetic interest in the composer. It was his idea to stage the tableaux of *Ma Mère l'Oye*, and make a divertissement of them for the Théâtre des Arts. Ravel, as his own carefree librettist, remembered the procedure he had conceived for his opera *Schéhérazade*, and adopted its episodic plot. His idea was to introduce *Petit Poucet*, *la Belle et la Bête* and *Serpentin vert*, into the tale of *La Belle au bois dormant*, by adding a prelude, a *fileuse* (or *Danse du Rouet*), and four interludes, designed to bind together the pieces of the early suite.

On the 21st January, 1912, *Ma Mère l'Oye* made a most successful appearance at the Théâtre des Arts. Never to have seen this youthful ballet in one of those mixed programmes which it shared with de Musset's *Fantasio* and Albert Roussel's *Festin de l'Araignée*, is to have missed the most wonderful treat the theatre could offer during the lovely evenings of that golden period. In the little theatre on the Boulevard des Batignolles, everything was carefully displayed to charm ear and eye. The performances of *Ma Mère l'Oye* had at this time an attraction which they did not reach again. M. Grovlez conducted the small orchestra to perfection. Drésa's *décors* were a miracle, and even more so were his costumes, which, in apparent confusion, evoked the fashions of the seventeenth century, and the ingenious exoticism of the eighteenth—Boucher's Chinese, Galland's negro pages. Jane Hugard's choreography was no stricter than the plot. It delighted Nijinsky, who told Ravel : " It's like dancing at a family-party."

Ravel could never leave the eighteenth century, to which his fancy constantly returned, without lingering for a while over the graces of the Restoration. He was in love with its conceits, its fashions and its furniture—and its frivolities as well, even while he ridiculed them. So, when Mlle Trouhanowa suggested dancing the *Valses Nobles et Sentimentales*, Ravel hastened to give them as a framework the salon of a fair cruelty of 1820—Adélaïde—and, as a plot, a typical story, where flower language should interpret the undercurrent of the intrigue. Symbolical flowers freed the ballet dancers from having to explain their feelings in mime. It was an ingenious idea, and admirably fitted for an intrigue which was nothing more than a lovers' battle, with its feints, ruptures and reconciliations. *Adélaïde, ou le langage des fleurs* was orchestrated in fifteen days in March, 1912, and appeared at Mlle Trouhanowa's *Concerts de Danse* at the Châtelet the following April 22nd.

Like Vincent d'Indy's *Istar*, Florent Schmitt's *Tragédie de Salomé*, and Paul Dukas' *Péri*, with which the programme was shared, *Adélaïde* was conducted by its composer. Ravel had not held a baton since the isolated performance of the Overture to *Schéhérazade*. His performance of *Adélaïde* was correct, if not masterly : " It isn't difficult," he admitted the first evening, " It's always in three-time . . ." And when we objected that the seventh waltz contained superimposed binary and ternary rhythms, he agreed that made it difficult ; " but when I get to that point, I just go round and round."

The delightful dancing of Mlle Trouhanowa and M. Bekefi, and the beautiful *décor* by Drésa, assured *Adélaïde* a favourable reception. But four gala performances were not enough to affect the musical public. The Opéra decided to produce the work during the difficult days of the war, on the 7th April, 1916 ; but the revival was not followed up, in spite of as good a production as circumstances would allow, with the ballerina Aïda Boni, and a *décor* borrowed from the *Fête chez Thérèse*.

The score of *Daphnis et Chloé* was partly finished in 1911. The Concerts Colonne performed parts of it, as did also the Russian Ballet, before a private audience. After the *Bacchanale* had been recast, the definitive edition was finished on the 5th April, 1912, according to the manuscript.

" Just as everything was ready," wrote Jacques Durand[1], the publisher of the work, " for putting the work under rehearsal at the Châtelet, I was told that M. de Diaghilev wanted to see me at my office . . . M. de Diaghilev informed me that the work did not entirely satisfy him, and that he was hesitating to go on with it. I used all my powers of persuasion to get M. de Diaghilev to continue with his original plan. M. de Diaghilev

---

[1] Jacques Durand : *Quelques souvenirs d'un éditeur de musique* (2nd series). (Durand and Co.), p. 16.

thought a little, then simply said to me : ' I'll do *Daphnis* ' . . .
During the rehearsals," continues Jacques Durand, " there
were fierce discussions between the librettist, the stage-
designer, and the interpreter of the name-part, Nijinsky. M.
de Diaghilev naturally took part in them. As these took place in
Russian, I could only make out the violence in the tone of their
voices. Questions of choreography were at stake ; their
opinions seemed to be diametrically opposed. I don't know
who finally carried the day. There must have been mutual
concessions ; but the rancour remained, and the rupture
between M. Fokine and M. de Diaghilev dated from that time,
a rupture which became official when the season of Russian
Ballet ended."

As may be gathered from this eye-witness account, the cradle
of the new-born work was not exactly surrounded by smiles.
It is easy to understand the reason ; planned during the excite-
ment of the first Russian seasons, when *Cléopâtre* and *Schéhérazade*
were to some extent reviving the ballet of action, *Daphnis*
suffered from its appearance among the Russian Ballets at a
time when the leaders were feverishly immolating what they
had once adored. The hindrance did not come entirely through
Ravel's music. It sprang from Fokine's miscalculated choreography, which made the reproduction of the most worn and
stereotyped actions of choreographic repertory inevitable. The
war dance, to take only one example, revived unnecessarily the
Danses du Prince Igor. It is also worth noticing that the choreographer, a slave to his technique, did not always make use of
the chances which the music gave him to modify his style.
The episode of Pan and Syrinx, which the composer intended
as a classical *pas de deux*, perfectly executed in accordance with
the rules for this kind of dance, is the occasion for a somewhat
insipid pantomime. On the other hand, the *pas seul* by
Daphnis, where Nijinsky made such graceful use of his goat-
herd's hook, the dance of the captive with bound hands—a
triumph for Karsavina—and, most of all, the dance of the
Nymphs, all betoken successful innovations. In this last
figure, the dancers only appear in profile in a series of sharply
contrasted attitudes, and the dance was to exercise a lasting
influence on the choreographers who succeeded Fokine in
Serge de Diaghilev's good graces. Nijinsky was the first to

be inspired by it in *L'Après-midi d'un Faune*, and later in *Le Sacre du Printemps*. Lastly, the *Bacchanale* derived its charm from its intense energy, let alone its remarkable originality.

Although the preparation was confused and of necessity imperfect, the performance was not unworthy of its interpreters : Nijinsky and Karsavina had the two leading parts, and Adolf Bolm and Mlle Frohman were both excellent in the episodic characters of Dorcon and Lycenion.

The musicians profited from the time which the dancers squandered in vain polemics. Under Pierre Monteux' direction, they had plenty of time to prepare, so that, on the evening of the first performance, which took place at the Châtelet, on the 8th June, 1912, nothing was really ready except the orchestra. Although it was magnificent, the *décor* by the painter Léon Bakst was not only at fault in imagining Greece from the standpoint of Trébizond or Téhéran, while the composer saw her through Louis David's eyes ; it also took no note of changes of perspective, a disadvantage which has never been able to be remedied in any of the various theatres where it has been used.

But the Russians have a genius for swimming against the tide. This first performance was excellent, in spite of being more or less of an improvisation, and *Daphnis* was received with a warmth, to which the press of 1912 bears accurate record. M. Robert Brussel considered *Daphnis et Chloé* " the most accomplished and poetic work which we owe to the artistic enterprise of M. Serge de Diaghilev . . . In the ordinary way we are dazzled by M. Ravel ; but this time we are stirred ; stirred, not because his manner is aggressive or haughty, but because it is infinitely gentle, fresh and tender, as it should be for such a subject." (*Figaro*, 9th June, 1912.)

" Ravel's art," wrote M. Emile Vuillermoz, " is astonishingly consolidated in this systematically plastic score. The composer has allowed the shape of his design to emerge in clear-cut lines . . . everything points to a balanced and consummate art. The last part of the work reveals even a happy carelessness, a kind of nonchalant mastery, sufficient to enrapture musicians who with consternation have seen a certain harshness and affectation become normal to the ironic Muse of *L'Heure Espagnole*." (Review of the S.I.M., 15th June, 1912.)

68

On the other hand, Gaston Carraud declared the rhythmic element is " extremely feeble in M. Ravel's poetic and picturesque score, and, as the development always relies on repetition, it gives an impression of marking time, instead of true movement . . ." (*La Liberté*, 11th June, 1912.)

As it was presented at the end of the season, the ballet only had two performances in its first year. It was successfully revived in 1913. After that it disappeared from the programmes of the Russian Ballet. Later on, M. Rouché acquired the *décor* for the Opéra in Paris, and engaged M. Michel Fokine to revise the choreography. The work remains in the repertory of the *Académie Nationale de Musique*, and appears there intermittently ; for *Daphnis* is supremely appropriate for large symphony concerts. The two orchestral suites which the composer made from the score contain, with the *Nocturne*, the *Lever du Jour* and the *Bacchanale*, the essential and best-written part of the work. In this form, *Daphnis* has toured the world.

CHAPTER VIII

Ravel in 1913—Clarens—Khovantchina—Ravel and Stravinsky—the Trois Poèmes de Mallarmé—Zaspiak-Bat—*the battle of* Le Sacre—*the* Trio—*the war—death of Madame Ravel.*

1913 : RAVEL WAS THIRTY-EIGHT. IN A FEW YEARS, WITH A zest and lightness of touch which he later regretted he could not recapture—like Jean-Philippe Rameau at the height of his glory—he built up the major part of his work. From 1905 to 1912, he gave measure of his ability in twenty compositions in which there was hardly any superfluous material. Most of them set the world of music by the ears. Nearly all of them have shaken the nonchalant public of music-lovers, who, as a result of two incomparably gifted and faithful interpreters, the singer Jane Bathori and the pianist Ricardo Viñes, have been drawn little by little to that art, " marvellously artificial and filled to the brim with a divine assurance," of which Nietzsche dreamed in the good old days of Wagner.

The garlands wreathed for him by the snobs, the eulogies of critics—and their perfidy—the voluntary, and more often involuntary homage paid to him on all sides by his juniors, his friends and, in time, his elders, in works which vie with each other in bearing the marks of his influence, made him realize that he was famous. But the same insensibility which he showed in face of failure, he now showed in his indifference to success. He avoided the easy ways in which fame always tries to trap her favourites. When everything invited him to repeat himself, he protested that it was unnecessary to cover ground already worked over, and set himself to fresh tasks. At a time when composers in France, England, Italy and elsewhere began to imitate him, the composer of the *Trois Poèmes de Stephane Mallarmé* was concerned with things far different from self-imitation.

Neither as man nor artist would he permit himself to be spoilt by success : the more he unburdened himself of his message, the more his natural reserve gave free rein to his sociability, courtesy and profound simplicity : " A gentleman," said Thackeray, " becomes more natural as he grows older." Naturalness was too inherent a characteristic of the Basque to be able to increase or diminish : but it was more in evidence.

Ravel was now living at No. 4, Avenue Carnot—quite close to the Place de l'Etoile, in a flat shared with his mother and brother. He no longer had side-whiskers as in the Compiègne days, nor the pointed beard of the *Histoires Naturelles* period, nor the square beard of the 1908 period. Since 1911 he favoured the clean-shaven features of his race, whose characteristics he shared both in his appearance and his art.

He was often to be found at the house of Mme de Saint-Marceaux, a friend of music and musicians, of Mme Edwards, the Egeria of the Russian Ballet, Mme Paul Clemenceau, M. and Mme Jacques Durand. Hardly a Sunday went by without him being found at Ida and Cipa Godebski's house in the Rue d'Athènes. He would have felt completely at ease there, if only there hadn't been the piano on which Ricardo Viñes insisted on playing his music . . .

Until then he had travelled little and had never gone out of Paris except in the summer, to breathe his native air at Saint-Jean-de-Luz. In the spring of 1913, circumstances brought him to the shores of the Lake of Geneva, the birthplace of the Ravel family.

Diaghilev was intending to stage *Khovantchina*, Moussorgsky's unfinished opera, which Rimsky-Korsakoff had completed in his own way, not always successfully. Several passages needed reorchestration and others needed rewriting with material taken from the original version. Although it was a thankless task, the Director of the Russian Ballet thought of increasing its interest by sharing the work between Ravel and Stravinsky. The latter had settled at Clarens, on the Lake of Geneva. Ravel therefore went to join his friend and collaborator, and spent March and April near him ; Stravinsky at the Hôtel du Mont-Blanc, Ravel at the Hôtel des Crêtes. The railway lay between them ; but the drudgery of *Khovantchina* was not the only thing to bring them together. Ravel discovered one of his colleague's compositions on Stravinsky's piano : the *Poèmes de la lyrique japonaise*, for voice and instrumental accompaniment. Ravel was tremendously interested in these poems, and planned to write for the same instrumental combination.

Stravinsky explained the genesis of the *Poèmes de la lyrique japonaise*. At Berlin he had met Arnold Schönberg, who had let him hear his *Pierrot Lunàire*. Stravinsky was at the opposite pole from the sombre kingdom where Schönberg wove his spells. But, though he remained a stranger to the spirit which governed the activities of this great distiller of the quintessential, he was by no means insensible to the subtle and exact methods of his art and the formulæ of his pharmacopœia.

Stravinsky found no difficulty in making Ravel share his enthusiasm. These two connoisseurs of the concrete agreed to lay hold on the good where they could find it, even in the music of a romantic who searched out the bad wherever he suspected it.

In this way *Pierrot Lunaire*, known only by report, and some of Schönberg's piano-pieces, spurred Ravel to undertake the *Trois Poèms de Stéphane Mallarmé* : "... Not only am I finishing *Khovantchina*," Ravel wrote to me on the 3rd April, 1913, " but I'm also composing two songs for voice, piano, string quartet, two flutes and two clarinets on Mallarmé texts. . . ." My attempt to guess the poems he had chosen produced the following answer on the 12th April : " You've only won a dozen macaroons, old man : you're right enough, the first is *Soupir*. But the lady's watch in finest quality rolled gold is meant for the man who guesses the second one, which is *Placet futile*. . . ." This second song was finished at Paris during the following month. The composer afterwards decided to complete the work by adding *Surgi de la croupe et du bond*, which was written the following summer and completed at Saint-Jean-de-Luz on the 27th August.

" I wanted," he said, " to transcribe Mallarmé's poetry into music, especially that preciosity so full of meaning and so characteristic of him . . . "[1]

The *Valses Nobles et Sentimentales*, M. Mantelli rightly observes, " summarize a tendency and open up a new development." Ravel was now busy following this up : the *Trois Poèmes de Stéphane Mallarmé* complete and exhaust his ceaseless

[1] Biographical sketch.

effort towards greater concentration and the reduction of matter and form to their bare essentials.

Following the poet's example, he aims to exclude all eloquence and rhetoric from his music, and isolate it from every extraneous element. Having reached the last degree of tension and dryness he creates his melody—for the melody is to master and dominate the harmony. The melodic line grows firmer. It no longer is magnetized by the harmony. It does not grant nearly so much to declamation which claims to impose on song the laws of speech.

Extreme purity, an inhuman yet sensitive union of absolute poetry and the most rigorous technique, sum up Stéphane Mallarmé—and also his composer.

The strange sublimation and unprecedented purification effected by the composer brought him to the peak of his art, the farthest limits of music. He knew well enough that he could not continue in such a rarefied atmosphere, nor permanently exist in these light constructions which have the brilliance, limpidity and hardness of diamond, but also the coldness of ice. " La région où vivre " of which the poet speaks is closer to the earth, that nourishing earth deeply penetrated by the roots of all kinds of reality, whether natural or supernatural—nearer one's native soil.

The Mallarmé poems were hardly finished when Ravel thought of composing a Concerto for piano and orchestra on Basque themes : *Zaspiak bat.* He had often successfully harmonized songs of many nationalities[1]. He was later on to apply the most eager ingenuity to an accompaniment for the Hebrew liturgy[2]. But, though he loved to adapt his art to the caprices of " natural music," as Felipe Pedrell calls it, he soon saw that he could not apply the opposite process and adapt popular songs to the demands of his own music.

This technician who had made a law of creative imitation for himself, categorically refused to graft anything upon the popular stock, following the example of his beloved Spaniards. The idea of subordinating folk-songs to laws incompatible with their essentials repelled him : " You cannot use popular song in this way," he later on declared to Father Donostia, that

[1] *Mélodies populaires grecques*, 1907 ; French and Italian songs, etc., 1910.
[2] *Kaddisch*, 1914.

73

distinguished specialist of Basque music ; "it does not lend itself to development."[1]

During his stay at Clarens, Ravel not only discovered Schönberg and the *Poèmes de la lyrique japonaise* : Stravinsky showed him his latest work, as yet unpublished. It was *Le Sacre du Printemps*. Ravel was seized with an enthusiasm for the Sacre which never abated. He foresaw that a thunderbolt was about to burst upon the musical world, as is shown in a letter to Lucien Garban, dated the 3rd March : "You must hear Stravinsky's *Sacre du Printemps*. I think it will be an event as great as the première of *Pelléas*."

True enough, on the 29th May, 1913, Ravel took part in that memorable battle of the *Sacre*, comparable in violence at least to the Battle of *Hernani*. While Florent Schmitt, in a voice of thunder, inveighed against "those tarts of the sixteenth arrondissement," a fashionable quarter in Paris, Ravel himself was at it hammer and tongs with one of the fair Bacchantes, who went as far as calling him "a dirty Jew" because he had courteously asked her to be quiet . . .

Although their natures were so different, Stravinsky and Ravel were able to understand each other admirably at that point in their respective developments represented by *Le Sacre* and the *Poèmes de Mallarmé*. Stravinsky's boldness controlled by prudent wisdom, his use of extreme tension whose limits he constantly explored ; ruthless outbursts in which, under cover of orchestral effect, the regulation of concrete values and the study of an organic style was worked out ; these characteristics of the young Russian master gained the sympathy, even the admiration, of his friend.

This mutual comprehension between the two great composers lasted up to the time of Stravinsky's *Rossignol*, and even beyond that to the performances of *Mavra* and *Renard*, which though they broke the mutual understanding, did not in any way destroy the esteem each felt for the other.

The Trio for piano, violin and 'cello, "whose first theme is Basque in feeling, was composed as it stands in 1914 at Saint-Jean-de-Luz . . ."[2]

[1] R. P. Donostia : "Hommage à Maurice Ravel" (*Gure Herria*, October to December, 1937).
[2] Biographical sketch.

74

The composition of the Trio at first proceeded parallel with the sketch for *Zaspiak bat*. This is shown by a letter of the 30th June written to Lucien Garban. Later on we shall see what value to attach to the composer's reference to the Basque feeling in the initial theme. The fact remains that the first movement of the Trio in A and possibly even more the *Pantoum*—show faint signs of a source of inspiration far more distant than the valleys of the Pyrenees. But this is not the root of the matter. As usual it concerns a formal problem here complicated by a technical one, as though the composer were working for a wager : in a Trio the principal stumbling-block of the form is the necessity of finding an equilibrium between pianoforte and string sonorities ; and only the infallible Saint-Saëns had managed to solve the antinomy.

So Ravel placed himself under Saint-Saëns' discipline, delighted to deal in material thus contrasted and to build upon recalcitrant foundations. He produced a finished work, at once severe and impassioned, in which each instrument is clearly outlined to the enhancement of the melody. In the most successful movements, especially the first and the *Passacaglia*, the incompatibility of opposing sonorities is solved with consummate lightness and distinction.

The fundamental coherence and purity of conception of the Trio in A shows a quality of mastery quite different from the frenzied melancholy which with infinitely less sureness of touch animates the Quartet. At the end of his life Ravel once compared the two works by declaring in my presence that without much regret he would exchange the technical knowledge of his mature work for the artless strength revealed in his youthful quartet. Coming from him, it is a somewhat surprising confession. None the less it shows that this little man of steel, so certain of himself and ordinarily so distrustful where " inspiration " was concerned, did not escape a state of mind common to most human beings, that of being aware of mysterious influences which escape all our analyses and without which we are powerless. He felt, nevertheless, that as his industry, which held no traffic with these secret forces, became stabilized and assured, so they lost their power. . . .

The war came upon Ravel at Saint-Jean-de-Luz while he was busy finishing the Trio. Although he had never had any particular illness, his extremely delicate constitution had exempted him from military service. All the same, he planned to join the forces in spite of the disapproval of his family and friends. His correspondence is full of his hopes and successive disappointments. Although he was usually a most negligent letter-writer, the war, separator of friends, drove him to confide to paper thoughts and feelings which he would never have spoken. The tone of his letters, light at first and deliberately mocking, gradually gave way to anguish during the course of three years, which forced the spoilt child from his beloved game, and brought him face to face with himself amidst suffering and want. I have been allowed to make substantial use of this correspondence.

On 26th September, 1914, he wrote to Lucien Garban : " . . . In five weeks I have done five months' work. I wanted to finish my Trio before joining up . . ."

And to myself, on the 1st October : ". . . I know only too well that in writing music I am working for my country ! At all events, I have been told it often enough in the last two months to convince me ; said in the first place to stop me volunteering, and later to comfort me in my failure. But they can't stop me and they can't comfort me. Must I before acting, wait, until a couple of uhlans arrive in the as yet non-existent garden of my dream-villa at Saint-Jean-de-Luz? Well, I've written a trio, like poor Magnard, and that's always a start. I'm nursing the wounded every week, too, which is pretty absorbing : it's extraordinary how many different kinds of things forty chaps can want in the course of one night !

" I am still writing music : it's impossible to continue with *Zaspiak bat* as the material for it is in Paris. It's a tricky business working at *La Cloche Engloutie*—this time, I think, I've got it—or to finish *Wien* (Vienna),[1] a symphonic poem. While I'm waiting for a chance to pick up the threads of my old task of Maeterlinck's *Intérieur*—a touching consequence of the alliance—I'm beginning two series of piano pieces : first, a French Suite[2]—no, it's not what you think— the Marseillaise doesn't come into it at all, but there'll be a forlane and a jig ; not a tango, though ; and secondly, a

[1] Origin of *La Valse*.
[2] First idea for the *Tombeau de Couperin*.

Nuit Romantique[1] full of spleen, with a hunt in hell, an accursed nun, etc. . . ."

" Cécile Sorel isn't here any more. Even Nouguès has left . . ."

Further efforts to join up proved fruitless. He persuaded himself, and endeavoured to persuade Paul Painlevé, that his light weight, which went against him in enlisting, ought at least to recommend him for flying.

He wrote to me at the Dardanelles, on the 14th December, 1915 :

" . . . I am not yet likely to get the *croix de guerre*, although I'm surrounded by the unspeakable dangers of a base camp (metro accidents, handcuff incidents, downfall of the government, etc.). Not to mention the fact that if trench life is infectious, I am at the moment well exposed . . . I am going to find another sort of funk-hole ; after more than a year of effort, I am going to join the Air Force. I have had my medical and follow-up examination : my heart and lungs are still good. Let us hope that the former will be sufficiently elastic to put itself into my stomach at the right moment . . .

" I haven't yet had the time—if this really is an excuse—to look over the orchestration of your songs. I will take them to the front—and I am sure that out there, I shall be able to work like you."

" May St. Theresa, patron saint of flyers, hear my prayer."

St. Theresa heard him but did not heed. He left his work on the *Trois Chansons* for mixed chorus, with words written by himself, the second of which makes simple and touching allusion to the sadness of war, and left for the front on the 14th March, 1916. As a last resource, he had joined up as a driver in the Motor Transport Corps. He was sent to the Verdun salient.

On the 27th March, he announced very sheepishly that he had " badly bashed up " his vehicle : " I was quite heart-broken, but my lieutenant has assured me that it's of no importance, and that I should see plenty more like that."

But he was as proud as any recruit in informing his war-godmother, Mme Fernand Dreyfus, four days later, that he was leaving : ". . . can't tell you where, disguised as though

[1] This plan was never realized.

for a fancy-dress ball and helmeted as if for a walk in the Rue de la Paix . . ."

On the 24th April, " a ridiculous accident—a skid in an attempt to avoid a *gendarme*," involved him in a visit to " a rehabilitation centre, fairly far back."

On the 2nd May, he wrote a short, typical note to his god-mother : " I think it would be wise to warn you that in case of any accident I have given them your name. Forgive me, I know that's not one of the pleasantest of duties. But Mme Delage, to whom the dreary task has fallen up to now, is no longer in Paris and it wouldn't be very convenient. Again a thousand apologies and thanks, but I won't say ' in antici-pation ! ' . . ."

The little he saw of the horrors of war did not arouse " fear " in him, but a wish to see more : " And yet, J'm a peaceful person ; I have never been brave. But there it is, I'm eager to have adventures. It has such a fascination that it becomes a necessity. What will I do, what will many others do, when the war is over ? . . ."

On the 21st May, he spent a restful Sunday in " the most lovely countryside : a torrential stream, with high banks ; waterfalls on the left and a little tunnel on the right where the tiny river is lost in a bower of leaves and white roses . . . All the time the hell over there goes on . . . I ate a meal here with some family—who have been evacuated—and made paper hens and ducks of breadcrumbs for the kiddies . . ."

A few days later, at an entertainment, he was asked to " play during the intervals. The comedy selected was *Tire au flanc* . . . I asked for a second." He wrote to Lucien Garban : " They wanted me to have something of my own sung, but when I thought of *Surgi de la croupe et du bond*, for instance, I felt it better to decline."

A certain league formed to " prohibit for a long period the performance in France of Austro-German works " appealed for his support, and received the following reply on the 6th June, 1916 : " To me it matters little that M. Schönberg, for instance, is Austrian by nationality. He remains a highly significant composer whose interesting discoveries have had a happy influence on some composers among our allies and among us as well. What is more, I am delighted that MM.

Bartok, Kodály and their disciples are Hungarian, and that they show it in their works with so much relish . . ." For this uncompromisingly classical Frenchman had a horror of the self-professed patriots and did not conceal his opinion of them.

Defeatists received the same treatment ; but the anger aroused in Ravel when confronted with the crassness or malice of mankind could not withstand the appeal of minute everyday happenings. " Oh the stupid pessimism of these idiots ' who aren't taken in ! ' This hidebound egoism, these mole-blind opinions . . . I'm interrupted by little squeaks : a poor little mouse has got caught in a trap meant for rats . . ."

On the 25th May, 1916, he had another medical examination on trying to get into the Air Force. The doctors pronounced him to be in a bad state : " It isn't only the carburettor that's affected. The motor itself only goes on three wheels. Even the speedometer has something the matter with it. Let's hope that the driving gear isn't going to go wrong now . . ."

His mother's health was on his mind and the idea that he was giving her cause for worry deeply affected him : " Thank you for the news you give me of my mother. You know the joy and comfort it gives me. My poor mother ! As long as she has no misgivings about me . . . she always thinks me well out of danger . . ."

This idea obsessed him, and with it he felt again the urge to return to his profession with an insistence that was surprising and almost tragic : " 4th June, 1916.—I'm really worrying only about one thing, not being able to kiss my poor mother . . . Yes . . . there is, still, something else—music. I thought I'd forgotten it. Several days ago my Muse returned, the tyrant. Can't think of anything else. I am sure that I should have been composing full steam ahead . . ."

4th July, 1916 : ". . . I have never felt so much a composer : I overflow with inspiration, all sorts of plans, chamber music, symphonies, ballets . . . I tell you, there's only one solution : the end of the war . . . or else my return to the front."

18th July : " . . . To hell with all except music . . . Of course, an artist may be intended for fighting, but certainly not for spending his life in barracks . . ."

Posted to a section of the motor depot at Châlons-sur-Marne, he arrived there on the 6th September and fell seriously ill. He wrote from hospital to ask for Alain Fournier's *Le Grand Meaulnes*, which he had not read. A spell of convalescence brought him back to Paris and provided him with the sad opportunity of being with his mother during her last days, as she died on the 5th January in the presence of both her sons.

The composer's friends found him sunk in a dumb stupor which resisted all expressions of sympathy. They had to try to distract a lost child who showed none of his feelings and whom nothing could comfort.

He spent some time in Paris with M. and Mme Fernand Dreyfus, then left for his Parc de Châlons on the 7th February. He was bored to death. So affectionate a person, who found communication with other people so difficult, could not endure the isolation : " I am all the more grateful to you for not having left me quite alone. Here I am more isolated than anywhere else, among friendly, gay companions, who seem miles away from me just now . . . Please give Edouard my love and tell him that I am not writing to him as I don't want to make his sadness harder to bear."

He vegetated one long month at Châlons, then dragged out some time in the depots near Paris before finding himself temporarily discharged. On the 20th June, 1917, he was installed at Frêne, near Lyons-la-Forêt, and from there he answered a letter of mine to say how glad I was to see him free : " I wish I could congratulate myself as sincerely . . . At last, I am working. That makes many things bearable . . . "

The same day he wrote to his friend Lucien Garban to ask him to send Liszt's *Etudes transcendantes*, *Mazeppa* and *Feux Follets*. " The model," Renoir used to say, " is only there for inspiration."

Le Tombeau de Couperin—Ballet pour ma fille—La Valse—*the story of a public honour*—*tastes and trends after the war*—L'Enfant et les Sortilèges—*Sonata for violin and violoncello*—*Sundays at the " Belvédère "*—*small works.*

" I HAD THEN (1917) COMPLETED ' LE TOMBEAU DE COUPERIN.' In reality it is a tribute not so much to Couperin himself as to eighteenth century French music in general."[1]

A tribute, not a pastiche. In the same way as a virtuoso practises by means of scales or vocal exercises which are not at first connected with the piece he is to perform, Ravel prepared himself for the composition of a French suite for piano by studying Listz's *Etudes transcendantes*—and *Mazeppa*.

As far as their form is concerned, the six pieces which make up the *Tombeau de Couperin*—*Prélude, Fugue, Forlane, Rigaudon, Menuet, Toccata*—certainly conform with the claims of their titles, but they are not obviously inspired either by the French clavecinists or by the man who was their chief. The only old master to whom any reference is made in the *Forlane* would seem to be Domenico Scarlatti. And if a contemporary model is needed for the central episode in the *Rigaudon*, or the elegiac *Menuet*, it would, I think, be Camille Saint-Saëns and Ravel himself—the Ravel of the *Menuet Antique* and the *Sonatine*. In thus plunging once again into creative activity he rediscovered something of the style of his twenties and by a trick of nostalgia, became a disciple of his earlier self, as if he wished to bid a smiling farewell to his youth.

Each of the pieces is dedicated to the memory of some friend killed at the front, but their graceful serenity makes them charming rather than melancholy. It seems that the composer felt that flowers left on graves are sad not in themselves, but because they are meaningless to the passers-by. The dedication of the Duo to the memory of Claude Debussy shows a similar preoccupation and restraint.

Le Tombeau de Couperin is a delightful easel picture. It would

[1] Biographical sketch.

81

count for little amongst Ravel's works were it not for its wonderful orchestration, completed two years later for the Concerts Pasdeloup. This transcription produces an effect that is virtually Mozartian. Strict necessity governs every move; with extreme economy and simplicity Ravel obtains translucence and variety of colour throughout the whole work; a precision in fact, which equals and possibly surpasses the most brilliant successes of his orchestral virtuosity.

Round about 1916, Mme Colette had written a fairy-tale which she first entitled *Ballet pour ma fille*. She submitted it to the Director of the Opéra. M. Jacques Rouché advised her to ask Maurice Ravel to set it. A copy of the book was entrusted to the Army Post Office but never reached its destination. After Ravel was demobilized, M. Rouché urged her to send a second copy of the *Ballet pour ma fille*. The composer at first refused it on the grounds that he had no daughter . . . But he admitted that it charmed him as much because it conjured up a familiar fairyland as by the faultless simplicity of its use of the supernatural. Nevertheless, he was frightened by the quantity and variety of the *tours de force* demanded by such a subject, and he suggested certain modifications so as to bring into high relief the fantastic element within this intimate environment and make the whole work more like American musical comedy. He eventually received the final text, and *L'Enfant et les Sortilèges* was accepted, if not already started.

"What shall I do, what will many others do after the war?" He felt weary and he suffered from insomnia. From 1918 to the end of 1919, he limited his activities to orchestration. He settled at Saint-Cloud, at 7 Avenue Léonie. He shared a pleasant villa there with his brother and M. and Mme Bonnet, his brother's colleagues, who made him a home and became almost a second family to him.

As his health did not improve, he was advised to seek mountain air. He spent the first weeks of 1919 at Mégève; but his insomnia, and what he called his neurasthenia, pursued him. It needed nothing less than a commission to set him going again. Serge de Diaghilev made a timely appearance with such a proposal, and also gave him a chance to realize a plan which he had cherished a very long time. He wanted to make a choreographic version of *Wien*, which in its early form dated back to 1906.

Ravel believed that Léonide Massine, at that time choreographer of the Russian Ballet, was obviously best equipped to breathe life into the sort of romantic *bacchanale* he had in mind. The plan began by pleasing Diaghilev, and he offered to produce the work at the close of the 1920 season, along with a certain *Pulcinella* which Stravinsky was writing.

While Stravinsky was on his way to Naples in pursuit of Pergolesi's volatile shade, Ravel found his way to the retreat in the Cévennes which had been offered to him by his friend Ferdinand Hérold. Cloistered at Lapras, near Lamastre, from December 1919 onwards, he busied himself in this wild solitude by reviving the ancient phantoms which the waltz always suggested to him, and by forcing them to obey his will. The elements of this choreographic poem for the part pre-date the *Rapsodie Espagnole*. The composer wisely held them in reserve, lest his power of synthesis should in the event fall short of his vaulting ambition. This vision tended to create innumerable forms of the waltz unified in a single clear structure, giving at once the illusion of controlled disorder and ordered freedom.

" . . . . I feel this work is a kind of apotheosis of the Viennese waltz linked, in my mind, with the impression of a fantastic whirl of destiny. I have given the waltz the setting of an Imperial Court, about 1855."[1]

Ravel had chosen to confine himself in a solitary place made almost tragically gloomy by winter, so as to work more easily and be free of importunate visitors. The first part of his stay was quite different from what he had hoped. The isolation intensified his grief, and on 26th December he wrote to Mme Fernand Dreyfus like an orphaned child : " I'm appallingly sad . . . She isn't here beside me any more, as she was in the days when I used to work away from Paris. And those wonderful Christmas Eves in the Avenue Carnot ! Ah well, I'm working, that's one thing."

The frenzy of work ended by taking him out of himself. On the 6th January, 1920, he wrote : " I'm waltzing frantically : I began orchestrating on the 31st December."

[1] Biographical sketch.

83

On the 16th January the press published the list of promotions and nominations for the order of the Légion d'honneur. In it appeared the name of " M. Ravel, Joseph-Maurice, composer of music." The news astonished those who knew Ravel and his continually reiterated, Baudelarian horror of decorations : " To consent to be decorated is to recognize that the State, or the ruling monarch, has the right to judge you, and to pay honour to you, etc."[1]

Ravel answered the telegram which I immediately sent by another : " Many thanks beg you contradict I refuse." He wrote to me by the same post : " Thank everyone. I have spent the day getting telegrams—none of them acknowledged : the rights of the composer of *Wien* are more important. What a mad business ! Who can have played such a practical joke ? I've written to Vuillermoz to ask him to have a statement issued, to wire me if he can take the matter up. . . . And *Wien* has to be finished at the end of the month ! But for that I would have left this evening."

The friends who " played this practical joke " did not mean any harm. The Minister of Public Instruction, M. Léon Bérard, considered it an honour to decorate Ravel. As the documents informing him to that effect had not been returned,[2] the friends in question thought it wise to convey the composer's acceptance to the Chief Secretary at the Ministry.

" You may imagine my despair ", Ravel wrote to me, when at last he was fully informed. " It's made me botch my orchestration all day. . . . Have you noticed how people who've got the Légion d'honneur are like the morphia addicts who go to any extreme, and even use guile, to make other people share their passion, possibly in order to justify it to themselves ? "

Yielding to his friends' entreaties to put the ribbon in his pocket and not make a scandal, Ravel at first did not make his decision known. In any case he had other things on hand. But when at length he expressly refused the ribbon the scandal was just as great, for this meant that the announcement of his withdrawal had to appear in the *Journal Officiel*.

So ended the third and last Ravel scandal. Later on, those

[1] Baudelaire : *Mon cœur mis à nu*, 1887.

[2] They did not arrive at Lapras until the 12th January, according to Ravel.

who disapproved of his attitude in the affair could listen to each other's invariably sneering comments to the effect that pride had been his only motive.

The brief argument of *La Valse* appears at the head of the score :

" Through the rifts of swirling clouds waltzing couples may be seen. One by one the clouds vanish ; a huge ball-room filled by a circling mass is revealed . . ."

It is a choreographic poem, written for a large, normally constituted orchestra, and made up of two great crescendos. The first follows a low vibration of the basses from which in characteristic rhythm springs the first summons to the dance ; it unfurls a long chain of waltzes which in their diversity reflect all the potentialities of the Viennese waltz : its insinuating charm and sudden brusqueness, its bursts of sensuousness, occasional nobility and striking dignity. Echoes of Schubert and more often of Johann Strauss blend at times with undertones pervaded by the memory of *Le Roi Malgré Lui* and the *Fête Polonaise*. But in the most successful parts, reminiscences of the *Valses Nobles et Sentimentales* dominate these fleeting evocations.

The second crescendo, shorter and much more vehement, gathers up these melodies and multiform rhythms, and crashes them together, furiously opposing and mixing them : a brutal, subtle development which does not really begin until the *stretto*, and is identified with it, returning at the end to the dominant key of D major.

The effect is very naturally to make the listener lose his balance. The whirl of the dance, everywhere heightened and accentuated, obsesses him with a sense of tragic destiny : he must whirl aimlessly, ceaselessly, and helplessly, until at last he succumbs to the lure of some unknown mælstrom.

This summons from the abyss is disconcerting : it is so unlike Ravel. A feverish romanticism, importunate and compelling, has, in no small measure, contributed to the extraordinary success of *La Valse*. Must this pathetic summons be admired as the climax of energy and art, the triumph of a prodigious imposture ? No : although the painting is skilful enough, it aims at dazzling rather than touching the heart. The drama is not in the picture : it is in the painter. For *La*

Valse is far from being one of Ravel's best compositions. The recapitulation is no less arbitrary for all the subtlety lavished on it. The orchestral sonorities are not here so nicely balanced as in other works. So much so, that conductors have each given their own interpretations of the piece, without always managing to preserve their own reputations—or that of the composer . . .

Even those who praised *La Valse* were a little uncertain in their formulæ. When Camille Chevillard first gave it at the Concerts Lamoureux on the 8th January, 1920, the enthusiasm of the best critics led them slightly off the track. And Th. Lindenlaub was not the only one who used Ravel's tour of Austria[1] to class *La Valse* as an occasional piece, a picture of post-war Vienna, animated by " the contrast between the light and careless dances of bygone days and the distressed and unhappy people who either dance from habit or to dull their sadness and hunger in dead delights. And this rising and mournful frenzy," Th. Lindenlaub goes on, " the struggle between the life-loving Johann Strauss and the will to destruction, takes on the phases of a *danse macabre*."

This commentary is inexact for it is too specific, but it is not without value if the action be transferred to the scene of the real tragedy, the very inner being of the artist.

In the case of this work, his first since the war, the composer at several points touched the limits of his territory. It seemed as though he fretted at the idea of not surpassing them. A prisoner of his very perfection, he tried vainly to break the chains he had so patiently forged, only to cover his hands in blood.

Ravel's *La Valse*, in short, reveals the advent of the "démon de midi " : a deep-seated impatience made his art tremble. He fabricated his enchantments with less detachment : he rebelled. He was really champing at the bit ; and though he may always have had " a smile on his lips," like Ramiro in *L'Heure Espagnole*, now that smile was one of pain.

Large orchestras have rendered meaningless the inexplicable scorn shown for *La Valse* by the Russian Ballet, who refused to stage it when the very excess of its virulence would seem to

[1] A journey which took place in October, 1920 ; later, in consequence, than the composition of the work.

commend it. For more than fifteen years, symphony concerts have wrangled over this brilliant piece. Along with *Boléro*, *La Valse* is Ravel's most successful work among the general public.

" Music has less to suffer from its immobility than from its mobilization," wrote Debussy during the gravest days of the war. But the war had finished and all the arts had been mobilized. Tastes and fashions were different. Every month showed signs of a new type of snobbishness. Those on the threshold of life woke up with all the disillusions of age. The rising generation, equally impatient to live and to create, made honest enough efforts to appear ruthless. Ravel was not the man to stop them. It was fine and good for youth to attack the greatest reputations.

Jean Cocteau, who up to now had been Reynaldo Hahn's librettist, had become the friend of Erik Satie who thereupon insinuated that the enemy they were looking for was Ravel. But Ravel did not give many openings to the Machiavellian tactics of the good man of Arcueil. His music was ample defence, and he himself, armed as he was with courteous indifference, did not acknowledge a hit. What was more, he was amazed that a generation justifiably so restless, did not react more strongly from his style, which put it in a most delicate position so far as he was concerned. Wagner—a pastmaster in such matters—was fond of saying that in art robbery can only justify itself by murder ; the converse is not true. Ravel, nevertheless, survived it all fairly well.

The rebirth of musical activity was everywhere apparent. Whatever he felt, Ravel was forced to resume an active life. He belonged to the small number of musicians who were counted on. Public opinion the world over took note of him ; he was ceaselessly harried. He realized quickly enough that he could no longer meet the demands of friendship and of public curiosity plus the exigencies of composition. So he decided to make his home sufficiently near to Paris to travel to and fro easily, but sufficiently far away to discourage unwelcome visitors. His choice fell on Montfort l'Amaury. He bought a house there—the " Belvédère "—which dominated the little town and the surrounding countryside. Léon-Paul Fargue described it as " an absolute toy, which also happens to be useful, one of those toys which spring surprises on you, with a single story in front and three at the back, a house which he has furnished and divided into compartments like a ship's cabin, or a work-basket, and which he has stocked with articles as precious and carefully chosen as a specialist's set of instruments.''

During the summer of 1920, Ravel was the guest of his friend Pierre Haour, at the Château de la Bijeannette, near Châteauneuf-en-Thimerais.[1] It was a hard-working holiday : ''. . . I am working at the opera with Colette—the final title has still not been settled . . . The work is in two parts and is remarkable for a mixture of styles which will be severely criticized, a fact which leaves Colette indifferent and me not caring a damn. I'm also working at a Duo for violin and 'cello in four movements. The piano alone stands idle and I'm afraid my virtuosity won't arouse the enthusiasm of the Viennese . . . ''

He was due to take part in a concert of his works in Austria. The price of fame was this obligation to appear more and more in public, at a time when his pianistic talent, which had never been outstanding, was suffering from evident lack of practice, and when, with an orchestra, his somewhat rigid baton showed the effects of an improvised technique.

He left for Vienna in October, and, on his return to Paris, was present on the 8th November for the première of *Le Tombeau de Couperin*, recast as a suite of dances by Jean Borlin and his company of Swedish dancers. The orchestra was conducted to perfection by D. E. Inghelbrecht. In deference to the wish of the composer, Pierre Laprade's *décor* and costumes did not so much evoke the period of Couperin, as that of Marie-Antoinette in order that the *tombeau* should be given a setting suited to the style of the tribute. A pleasant production, and certainly a very successful one ; Ravel was able to conduct the hundredth performance of the ballet on the 15th June, 1921.

On the 12th December, *La Valse* had its first hearing at the Lamoureux ; on the 27th January, *L'Heure Espagnole* was revived at the Monnaie in Brussels.

L'Enfant et les Sortilèges had found its title, but its music was still at the Arithmetic scene.   Ravel shut himself up in Montfort

[1] In the department of Eure-et-Loir.

A Sunday at 'Belvédère' : left to right and top to bottom : Hélène Jourdan-Morhange, Mme. Roland-Manuel, Andrée Vaurabourg, Mme. Lucien Garban, Arthur Honegger, Germaine Tailleferre, Mme. X, Madeleine Picard, Lucien Garban, Ravel, Mlle. Pavlovski, Mme. Hélène Casella (Roland-Manuel).

Maurice Ravel at Lyons, 1922 (Roland-Manuel).

Maurice Ravel, Hélène Jourdan-Morhange, and Ricardo Viñes (Mme. Jourdan-Morhange).

Ravel orchestrating the *Tableaux d'une Exposition* in Lyons, 1922 (Roland-Manuel).

Maurice Ravel on the balcony of his
'Belvédère', at Montfort-l'Amaury (Roland-
Manuel).

The 'classe Ravel,' in 1922 : from left to right Maurice Delage, Maurice Ravel,
and Roland-Manuel (Roland-Manuel).

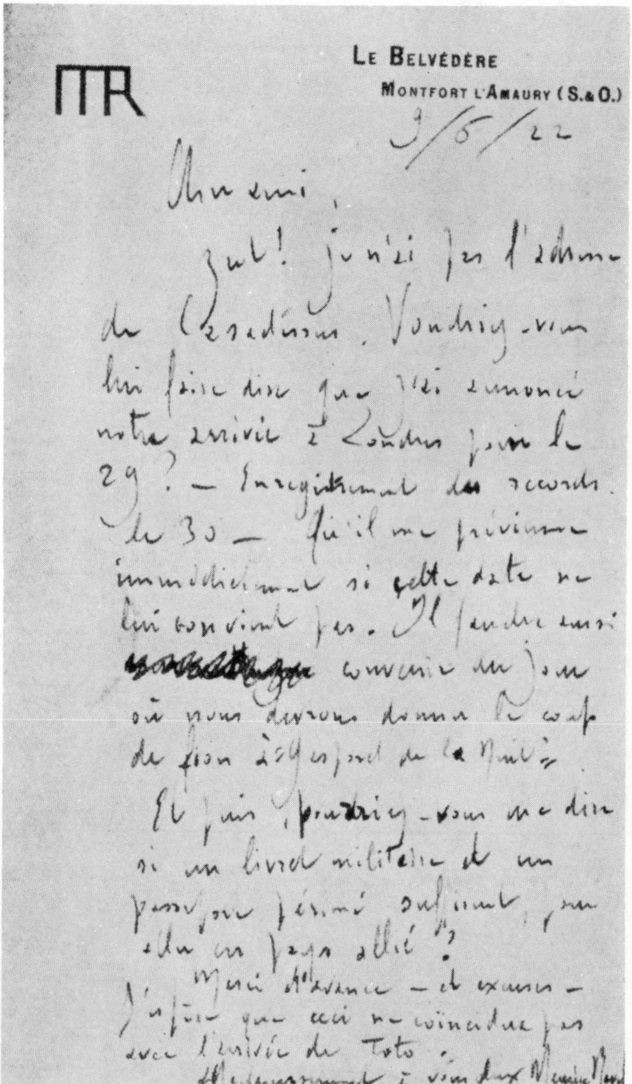

9/5/22

Cher ami,

Zut! je n'ai pas l'adresse de l'Aeolian. Voudriez-vous lui faire dire que j'ai annoncé notre arrivée à Londres pour le 29? — Enregistrement des records le 30 — qu'il me prévienne immédiatement si cette date ne lui convient pas. Il faudra aussi [illegible] convenir du jour où nous devrons donner le coup de fion à Gaspard de la Nuit.

Et puis, pourriez-vous me dire si un livret militaire et un passeport périmé suffisent pour aller en pays allié?

Merci d'avance — et excuses — j'espère que ceci ne coïncidera pas avec l'arrivée de Toto.

Affectueusement à vous deux Maurice Ravel

A letter from Maurice Ravel to Roland-Manuel.

and worked uninterruptedly at the composition of the Duo which later on became the Sonata for violin and 'cello. Few of his compositions caused him so much effort : on 22nd September, 1921, he wrote " this devil of a Duo is giving me agony." On the 29th, he " began to see a little daylight in the Duo" On the 3rd February, 1922, " I'd finished the Duo. And then I began to notice that the *scherzo* was much too highly developed . . . so I started it all over again, using fresh material . . . "

The Sonata was finished at last. Ravel considered that this work, which used the most modest apparatus, " marks a turning point in my evolution." " The reduction to essentials," he says, " is carried to extremes. The fascination of harmony is disregarded. A more and more marked reaction in the direction of melody is apparent."[1]

The Sonata for violin and 'cello is a hard, taut work, and the two instruments emulate each other in rejecting all the intrinsic charm expected of their respective timbres. The first movement sets out four themes with great simplicity. Two of them appear throughout the whole work, which is cyclic. The sturdy, vituperative and biting *scherzo* shows to a marked extent the violence and raucousness which from now on seemed to draw the composer of *La Valse*. An emotional *andante* divides the *scherzo* from the *finale* : a serene episode infused with the rarefied clarity of exquisite melodies. The structure of the *finale* is related curiously to the *rondo* of a Mozart piano sonata (F major, 1786). The two instruments become the actors in a fantastic comedy whose strange turbulence is deftly inserted into the Mozartian framework.

This remarkable sonata, bristling with virtuosity and a lyricism which spits like an angry cat, is one of the most significant—and the least flattering—works in Ravel's new manner. Its harsh impetus will occasionally be found in his later compositions. The violin and 'cello Sonata was followed by a period of tranquillity.

The composer's intimate friends had at this time the habit of meeting on Sundays at Montfort l'Amaury. Newcomers were astonished at the simplicity with which the great composer did the honours of his " Belvédère " with the joy of a schoolboy

[1] Biographical sketch.

on holiday. Who could fail to be surprised and charmed by his smiling gravity when he displayed his collection of trinkets and knick-knacks of the time of Charles X and Louis-Philippe ?

The new friends mingled with the old " Apaches " in an atmosphere of discreet gaiety. An unwritten law banned serious topics and æsthetic discussions. The violinist Hélène Jourdan-Morhange, the singers Madeleine Grey and Marcelle Gerar ; Mlle Madeleine Picard, Mlle Pavloski, Germaine Tailleferre ; Maurice Delage, Maurice Tabuteau and their wives : the painter Luc-Albert Moreau, the sculptor Léon Leyritz, who had made a very beautiful bust of the master of the house, and later on M. and Mme Jacques de Zogheb, M. and Mme Jacques Meyer, the doctor Robert Lemasle, the composer Manuel Rosenthal—all these in turn were frequent guests at the " Belvédère " at Montfort l'Amaury.

During the summer of 1922, the composer returned to Lyons-la-Forêt. While he was staying with me, he orchestrated Moussorgsky's *Tableaux d'une Exposition*, commissioned by Serge Koussevitsky and interrupted in order to write the *Berceuse on the name of Fauré* for violin and piano, which was to be his contribution to a collective tribute organized by the *Revue Musicale* in honour of the master of *Pénélope*. It was then that Ravel pursued the airy spirit of Fournier's *Grand Meaulnes* in the forests of Rambouillet and Lyons ; but the fair prey stole away and escaped him.

The concert tours multiplied and tired him without curing his insomnia : Amsterdam, Venice, a return to Montfort towards the end of December. February and March, 1923, saw him at Saint-Jean-de-Luz. He had a respite there before leaving for London to conduct *Ma Mère l'Oye* and *La Valse*, and from there he modestly informed his friend and interpreter Hélène Jourdan-Morhange that " . . . according to the newspapers I am at least a good, if not a great, conductor. I hadn't expected as much as that . . ."

On his return to Montfort in August, 1923, he began a sonata for violin and piano : " . . . It won't be very difficult," he wrote to Hélène Jourdan-Morhange, " and it won't sprain your wrist." But this sonata, whose composition was frequently interrupted for other work, only saw the light of day in 1927. He wrote it slowly in accordance with a habit cultivated as a technique. He was bothered by the thought of approaching claims he would have to meet : during the summer of 1923, Raoul Gunsbourg, who wanted to produce *L'Enfant et les Sortilèges* at Monte Carlo, had managed so well that he had succeeded in wresting from a weary composer what he could never have obtained from the normally negligent one : a contract, duly signed and sealed, obliged Ravel to finish the score by the end of 1924.

The beginning of the year had, however, seen the composition of *Tzigane*, " a virtuoso piece in the style of a Hungarian rhapsody "[1] for violin and orchestra, dedicated to the violinist Jelly d'Aranyi, and also a piece of small compass but great significance—*Ronsard à son âme*[2] where, when depicting an object, in this case a monument, Ravel's music, for the first time, makes " what is primarily his own confession as an artist."

But he had to dry this first tear, and begin life again : " I'm not leaving the grindstone or seeing anybody, I'm going out just enough to prevent me from passing out ; if *L'Enfant et les Sortilèges* doesn't get finished it won't be my fault."[3]

---

[1] Biographical sketch.
[2] Composed for *Le Tombeau de Ronsard* at the request of the *Revue Musicale*.
[3] Letter to Hélène Jourdan-Morhange.

L'Enfant et les Sortilèges—*the* Chansons madécasses—*Sonata for violin and piano* —Ravel's discovery of America—*the wager on* Boléro.

" L'ENFANT ET LES SORTILÈGES "—A LYRICAL FANTASY IN TWO parts—is a fairy-story brought up-to-date, if not directly inspired by Andersen. Its plot is simple enough : weary " of the uneventful happiness and tranquillity of the quiet life," a naughty little boy breaks up the furniture and tortures the animals in malicious fury. Then the outraged household gods take their revenge. The furniture comes to life and defies him. His first love. the Princess of the fairy tales, shows herself only to bid him farewell.

In the second scene, the damaged trees, tormented squirrels and skinned tree-frogs in turn come to threaten him ; but he has dressed the wounds of a small injured squirrel. The animals forgive him and take him as far as his house, where his mother is waiting for him.

This familiar cautionary tale for children gave Ravel an ideal chance to rediscover the world of enchantment, to move and be moved in a world free from the tyranny of human passion, to act in a play which revolutionizes emotional values as easily as the laws of perspective ; where teapots are the size of men ; where cats talk of love and squirrels of redemption ; and where, in revenge, the race of Adam has as its sole representative a cruel and barbarous child.

We left the composer grappling with the difficulties imposed by the strength of a perfect and established technique. We have seen Ravel furiously impatient to get outside Ravel or to get the better of him. In the middle of *L'Enfant et les Sortilèges*, which testifies to no less an intention, it sometimes seems that the composer has succumbed to the necessity of telling his own story in music : " I don't care, I don't care— and I'm not hungry. I'd much rather be left alone . . ." How can anybody fail to recognize, in the wanton destruction of the little destroying fury who tears the heart out of clocks and arouses the hostility of familiar objects, the Ravel of the dry virulent Duo ?

Ostensibly Mme Colette's story fulfilled the composer's fondest hopes, not to speak of fulfilling the conditions of a good libretto. I say ostensibly, because the reader's outlook must be circumscribed if he is to enjoy to the full the collusion of the enchantress and her illusionist. One would look in vain for two more original spirits. One would be hard put to it to find two more incompatible. The world of fancy which they transform, each in their fashion, into living matter, is tamed by Mme Colette but subdued by Ravel. And the conflict of spontaneous poetry and reflective music would inevitably have ended in catastrophe if the poet, hiding behind her colleague, had not muzzled eloquence, cut down phrases to a minimum, and the plot to one suitable for ballet. In this form, and by the very tenuousness of its structure, the work calls for symphonic treatment, but its unassuming manner does not hide its arbitrary qualities.

It poses a set of delicate problems to the composer, producer, scene-painter and dress-designer, and a solution is only really reached in the music. Music may only part the gauze veils of fairyland a fraction, but the attempt rivets our attention and everything else is a distraction.

In *L'Enfant et les Sortilèges*, the writing more often than not, is commendably modest : the introduction, the *pastorale*, the scene of the Princess and practically the whole of the second part are full of this will to simplify, and the need to make the sound-texture lighter—to aerate it, as it were—which represents the most deliberate movement yet made by Ravel towards stripping bare his material. He pursues the path opened up by the Duo and *Ronsard à son âme*. Once again, the melody improves as the work becomes less complex : " . . . The melody, a dominant preoccupation, has a theme which I have chosen to treat in the manner of an American musical comedy," says the author. " Mme Colette's book allows for such free treatment. Here it is the vocal line that should dominate. The orchestra, though it does not scorn virtuosity, is nevertheless of secondary importance."[1]

[1] Biographical sketch.

This search for a less rich texture, less likely therefore to perturb or mislead the ear, frees the composer from any trace of ambiguity still left in his art. A persistent and fine boring drill succeeds in piercing the wall of a prison which all the furies of *La Valse* had not so much as shaken. No matter whether this candour be gained by underground or frontal attack, it gives a surprising brightness and contrast to the orchestration of *L'Enfant et les Sortilèges*. In this final repudiation of thematic development, and the break-up of the continuity of recitative, Ravel manages to free his music from whatever elements of subjectivity it still contained.

L'Enfant et les Sortilgèes appeared for the first time in March, 1925, at the Monte-Carlo Opera House, under the direction of the great conductor Victor de Sabata. Mlle Gauley (as the Little Boy), MM. Fabert (as the Little Old Man) and Warnery (the Clock and the Cat) were at the head of a cast which had as many as eighteen important rôles. The success was an "astounding" one according to the distinguished critics present at these first performances. The following year, on the 1st February, 1926, the Opéra-Comique gave the dress-rehearsal of the work.

M. Albert Wolff conducted the orchestra very ably, and the part of the Little Boy was admirably interpreted by Mlle Gauley. The majority of the female parts and all the male ones came up to expectation. (Mlles. Calvet, Kamienska, Féraldy, Sibille, Réville, Ducuing, Prazères ; MM. Bourdin, Guénot, Hérent, Génin.)

Though it was well received in Paris by the audience at the final rehearsal, *L'Enfant et les Sortilèges* had a stormy first-night. The cat scene roused some of the audience to fury, and others to laughter, while the effects borrowed from music-hall technique had a varying reception. To make up for it, the critics had never before been so loud in praise of any work by Ravel.

M. Vuillermoz was particularly impressed by "its atmosphere of tenderness and delicate pantheism, the early signs of which appeared in *le jardin féerique* in *Ma Mère l'Oye*. The whole of the end of the second act and the touching lament of the Princess have the distinction of being unusual confessions from Ravel." (*Excelsior*, 3rd February, 1926.) M. Henry Malherbe, in *Le Temps*, hailed *L'Enfant et les Sortilèges* as " a work of genius." A few critics were less enthusiastic : André Messager, whom Ravel admired but who did not reciprocate this feeling, reproached the composer for offering sacrifice to imitative music. But Arthur Honegger, in *Musique et Théâtre*, had already shown that the chief bone of contention, the cat-duet, could be both justified and explained. He called it " the most miraculous part of the score." " Naturally," wrote Honegger, " Ravel was not concerned with imitating the mewing of cats ; but he has so used it as to build up a melodic line deriving from it. In it is to be found the whole crux of so-called ' imitative ' music."

For two seasons *L'Enfant et les Sortilèges* appeared on the posters of the Opéra-Comique, but it had no more than fifteen performances. In addition to the mediocrity of the scenic design and *décor*, the end of the first scene was usually greeted with the " odd commotions " of a public whose evident sincerity exceeded its musical taste. At one of the last performances of the work, Ravel noticed that one of the occupants of the next box was energetically trying to hiss unsuccessfully, so he discreetly handed me a hollow key, which he had on him, entreating me to lend it to the protester . . .

" In addition to the Sonata and the *Chansons madécasses*," wrote Ravel on the 7th August, 1925, " I have consented to do an operetta—to be finished by the end of the year . . . " But the operetta was to remain as a project, and the *Chansons madécasses* and the Sonata were not finished till the next year.

On the 1st February, 1926, at the time of the dress rehearsal of *L'Enfant et les Sortilèges*, Ravel was in the train for Stockholm, the first stage of a tour of Scandinavia, England and Scotland. On the 4th he wrote to Hélène Jourdan-Morhange : " I'm leaving for Oslo. *L'Enfant*, according to *Le Temps*, seems to be having a rough passage." He returned to Montfort at the beginning of March and settled down to the *Chansons madécasses*, which he finished the next month.

Being a confirmed admirer of *bibelots* dating back to the Revolution, Directoire, Empire and Restoration, Ravel bought, between an 1820 Gothic clock and an Etruscan teapot, a first-edition of Evariste Parny. As he was looking through the poem *Fleurs :*

95

L'ognon préfère un sol épais et gras
Un sol léger suffit à la semence
Confiez-lui votre douce espérance,
Et de vos fleurs les germes délicats . . .[1]

he had a cablegram from America from the 'cellist Kindler asking him to compose a song-cycle for Mrs. Elisabeth S. Coolidge, with accompaniment " if possible " for flute, 'cello and piano. Always happy, in true Mozartian fashion, to adjust himself to a task that had been determined for him by another's will, the composer tenaciously went on reading Parny, having made up his mind to provide an accompaniment of piano, flute and 'cello for the words of the ' French Tibullus.' Delighted by a peculiar, exotic quality which entirely suited his tastes, as local colour was virtually excluded, his choice fell on the fifth, eighth and twelfth *Chansons madécasses*.

This chance request inspired the best of his post-war chamber-music : " I think that the three *Chansons madécasses* bring into being a new, dramatic, almost erotic element, resulting from the subject-matter of Parny's poems. They form a sort of quartet with the voice as the chief instrument. Simplicity is all-important. The independence of parts (shown there) is more obvious in the Sonata (for violin and piano) . . ."

The music is reduced to its essential, primitive elements, melody, rhythm and pitch, and is entirely free from the tyranny of harmony. Ravel amuses himself by pursuing the same road as jazz composers, though in the opposite direction ; he discovers negro music through syncopated rhythms and the juxtaposition of major and minor thirds, and allows his 'cello to imitate the calabash by pizzicato harmonies ; while his lyric genius, in love with the fair Nahandove, forsakes the enchantments of magic and comedy for this exotic Venus, and for once extols the delights of earthly pleasures.

The Sonata for Violin and Piano is a twin to the *Chansons madécasses*, so completely and so effectively does it seem to be made up of the same substance, particularly in the first and most successful movement. This independence of instrumental parts to which Ravel was so obviously attracted, shows itself in the

---

[1] The bulb prefers a thick luxurious soil,
A light soil is sufficient for the seed,
Entrust to it your tender hopes
And of your flowers the delicate buds . . .

juxtaposition of piano and violin ; as Ravel puts it, " essentially incompatible instruments, which not only do not sink their differences, but accentuate incompatibility to an even greater degree."[1] At times the piano gives the violin a small, edged descant, which makes the listener hesitate about the tonal sense of the passage.

The second movement is a carefully individualized *blues* which is strangely reminiscent of the dialogue between the Teapot and the Cup in *L'Enfant et les Sortilèges*. The stereotyped formulæ of the genre and the traditional jazz interpolations are mordantly mingled with the Ravelian *melos*, and continue beneath a fine network of semi-quavers, tirelessly spun by the violin in the third and last movement—*perpetuum mobile*.

1927 saw the publication of two miniatures, the first, *Rêves*, a setting of a poem by Léon-Paul Fargue, expressing an outlook similar to that of the *Chansons madécasses*, and the Sonata. The other is a *Fanfare* to preface a children's ballet written by several composers jointly at the request of Mme René Dubost : *L'Eventail de Jeanne*. It is a lilliputian flourish which begins like the buzzing of troops of insects and rises to its climax in the style of the *Twilight of the Gods*.

In the early part of 1928, Ravel discovered America, or, more accurately, Canada and the United States, during a four-month tour, which, following an extravagant itinerary, took him from New York to Chicago, from San Francisco to Los Angeles, then to Seattle and Vancouver ; from Minneapolis to New York, New Orleans, Houston, the Grand Canyon of Colorado, Buffalo, New York and Montreal, not to speak of short expeditions to Boston, Cambridge and Cleveland.

" I am seeing magnificent cities, and enchanting country ; but the triumphs are tiring," he wrote to Hélène Jourdan-Morhange. " At Los Angeles, I eluded people. Besides, I was dying of hunger . . ." All the same he assured Mme Fernand Dreyfus that he " had never felt so well as during this crazy tour. I have finally discovered the reason for it : it is because I have never led a reasonable enough life . . ." At length he boarded the *Paris*, and on the 27th April, he was back home again.

[1] Biographical sketch.

97

Before leaving for America, the composer had been sounded by Mme Ida Rubinstein about a ballet she wanted him to do. At the time Ravel did not want to be involved in the composition of an original work, but he willingly agreed to orchestrate some pieces of Albeniz. Through his usual indolence, time elapsed between the plan and its execution. But for once, the course of events was to justify his nonchalance. While he took his ease in Saint-Jean-de-Luz, where he was spending July, Mme Ida Rubinstein learnt that the heirs of Albeniz had given the exclusive orchestration rights of Albeniz' works to the conductor Arbos—all the more reason for staying on at Ciboure. Now it so happened that the good-natured Arbos had heard about it, and protested that he would gladly renounce his rights in favour of somebody like Ravel. But Ravel now found that it was very late to begin work, for Mme Rubinstein's ballets were due for the beginning of the season. " After all," he said to his friends, " I would have orchestrated my own music much more quickly than anyone else's." But he had yet to write that music.

Ravel returned to Montfort, stubbornly intending not to compose but to orchestrate. He had no desire to find an incentive for composition : he wanted a subject for orchestration. In this way *Boléro* came into being.

" In 1928, at the request of Mme Ida Rubinstein, I wrote a *Boléro* for orchestra. It is a dance whose pace is very steady and uniform, as much in the melody and harmony as the rhythm, which the side-drum beats out all the time. The orchestral crescendo provides the only variation."

With overwhelming persistence and no developments or modulations, except in the coda, *Boléro* repeats two stereotyped dance-themes, supported by commonplace harmonies. Its entire interest as a *tour de force* consists in the management of the orchestral crescendo, which becomes more brightly and variously coloured every time the themes return—" an astonishing merry-go-round of tone-colours," to use M. Mantelli's apt description. *Boléro* first appeared in Mme Rubinstein's ballet repertoire at the Opéra on the 20th November, 1928, in company with *La Valse*, and the production was pleasing.

Those friends of the composer who, a few days before, had been present at the first orchestral reading under Walther Straram did not expect, any more than the composer, the astonishing success of this piece of sleight-of-hand. I can still hear Ravel telling us : " This is a piece which the big Sunday Concerts will never dare include in their programmes ; what do you make of it ? "   And each of us thought exactly as he did about it.

The triumphant fate of *Boléro* is well known. On the heels of the " great Sunday Concerts," where the work immediately received an immense ovation, large and small orchestras everywhere, appropriated it. It inspired films. Gramophone and radio repeated it all day long. The butcher boy whistled it and all the street answered him. So that the composer of the *Valses Nobles et Sentimentales* became popular through what he rightly considered to be a joke on the part of his genius.

" I am not going to stir and I'm working like mad till mid-October," Ravel wrote on the 10th August, 1928, before flinging himself into the orchestration of *Boléro*. " After that, I ought simultaneously to be in Oxford—to take the degree of Doctor *honoris causa*—in Spain and at the Opéra where Ida Rubinstein is performing *La Valse* and a new work which I may possibly have finished by then."[1]

The journey to Oxford and the tour of Spain took place slightly later on. During this period Ravel was increasingly fêted. He was in demand everywhere, both on the dais, and as the interpreter of his famous *Boléro* which he conducted with a stiff gesture, and at a steady, fairly slow, uniform pace. As he was never unduly put out by people or situations, he did not scruple to reprove Toscanini on one occasion, in the tones in which one reproves a schoolboy, for the speed at which he took *Boléro*.

It was not a question of success giving him the haughty frigidity of those who think they are important ; for he had never been so simple or childlike. And though it was likely that he was increasingly anxious about his health, he was still just as good-tempered. For every day, for no obvious reason, he felt more fatigued, and he suffered from severe insomnia. He was told that he did not lead a healthy life. He was reproached for his nocturnal habits, dating so far back that they seemed to be an essential part of his genius : it was in the

[1] Letter to H. Jourdan-Morhange. *Boléro* was finished about the 6th October.

course of his night-walks, that he worked out fresh projects and watched while new ideas slowly matured.

Periodically he would leave the solitude of Montfort ; a *pied-à-terre* was made in the house his brother Edouard shared with the Bonnet family, at Levallois, 16 Rue Chevallier, almost opposite the one where he had written the *Histoires Naturelles*, *L'Heure Espagnole* and *Gaspard de la Nuit*. His friend Léon Leyritz decorated the flat in a modernistic style that makes a pleasing contrast to the furnishing at the ' Belvédère.' His family and friends surround him and give him every attention. Mme Jacques Meyer and Mme Marguerite Long share his company with his brother, Maurice and Nelly Delage, and Manuel Rosenthal. He was still the most delightful of companions, the simplest, most fastidious of friends—and the most demanding ; but he no longer had the unheeding, detached look which up to then had showed in his smile and bearing : a look which was peculiarly alert yet ingenuous.

He was full of plans but was fretting at not being able to give form to them. All the same, he was determined to write an opera on Joseph Delteil's *Jeanne d'Arc*, discussed it at length with M. Jacques Rouché, and was concerned about the *décor* which he wanted to entrust to Jean Hugo. He also entertained the idea of a concerto, which at first he thought of playing himself, but later decided to write for Marguerite Long.

While he hovered between these alternations of hope and despair, he received and accepted a commission for a concerto for left hand alone from the Viennese pianist Wittgenstein (who had lost his right arm through the war.)

CHAPTER XI

The two Concertos—Don Quichotte à Dulcinée—*the final years*—*his illness*—*death of Maurice Ravel.*

SEPTEMBER 1929 : CIBOURE, SAINT-JEAN-DE-LUZ, BIARRITZ, AND the whole Basque coast fêted Maurice Ravel—inevitably there were symphony concerts, and pelota tournaments and *fandangos* as well. The Rue du Quai at Ciboure was re-christened the Quai Maurice Ravel. The composer was as much moved by these demonstrations as he was embarrassed at finding himself their object. He never had words for such occasions. He did not know how to return friendly demon-strations. A prophet in his own country, he felt himself out of his element for the first time . . .

He was grappling with two works for which the publisher was waiting and which he had to write simultaneously. To use his own words :

" It was an interesting experience," he told a *Daily Telegraph* correspondent [1], " to conceive and realize the two Concertos at the same time. The first, which I propose to play myself, is a concerto in the strict sense, written in the spirit of Mozart and Saint-Saëns. I believe that a concerto can be both gay and brilliant without necessarily being profound or aiming at dramatic effects. It has been said that the concertos of some great classical composers, far from being written *for* the piano, have been written *against* it. And I think that this criticism is quite justified.

" At the beginning, I meant to call my work a ' divertisse-ment,' but afterwards considered that this was unnecessary, as the name Concerto adequately describes the kind of music it contains. In some ways my Concerto is not unlike my Violin Sonata ; it uses certain effects borrowed from jazz, but only in moderation.

" The Concerto for left hand alone is quite different, and has only one movement with many jazz effects ; the writing is not

[1] Quoted by Alfred Cortot : *La Musique française de piano*, Vol. II, page 46.

so simple. In a work of this sort, it is essential to avoid the impression of insufficient weight in the sound-texture, as opposed to a solo part for two hands. So I have used a style which is much more in keeping with the consciously imposing style of the traditional concerto.

"After an introductory section pervaded by this feeling, there comes an episode like an improvisation which is followed by a jazz section. Only afterwards is one aware that the jazz episode is actually built up from the themes of the first section."

Begun in 1930, the composition of the two Concertos was finished in the autumn of the following year. The Concerto for the left hand was the first to be completed, and was performed at Vienna on the 27th November, 1931. But it was Paris which was first to hear the Concerto in G major; the composer sent it to Mme Marguerite Long on the 11th November, 1931, and Ravel conducted its first performance on the 14th January, 1932, at the Salle Pleyel.

The Concerto in G major follows out the composer's intention very closely. It is a virtuoso " divertissement," brilliant, clear and light, with sharp contrasts which navigate with Mozartian ease the classic difficulties presented to free recapitulation by the formal sonata.

The initial *allegramente*, with its astounding vigour, imposes a hard and energetic harmonic " climate " upon melodic lines which, in their delicacy and capacity for easy adjustment, are related not so much to the Sonata for violin and piano as to *Ma Mère l'Oye* and *Ondine*.

Some critics have professed to find the contrast of the *adagio assai* and the two movements which bound it incongruous. In a work free of the strictures of " cyclic " writing, it is as legitimate a contrast as the precisely similar example in the *larghetto* of Mozart's Clarinet Quintet, which Ravel took as his model. The *adagio* is really a *lied* whose calm contemplation brings it unusually close to Fauré's musings. The composer confessed to Mme Long, when she praised the free development of the leisurely melody, which she felt came so naturally, that he had written it " two bars at a time, with frequent recourse to Mozart's Clarinet Quintet." But, once again, the original had become absorbed into the pastiche and entirely disappeared.

The conclusion is heralded by a terse *presto*, at once brilliant, brief and scintillating—a chase goaded by galloping fanfares and not to be halted by the nasal tattoo of jazz. It is a violent struggle between metre and rhythm—the apotheosis of tonality.

Nothing shows Ravel's supreme technical mastery better than the complete dissimilarity of these two works conceived and written at the same time : the disparity between their styles corresponds to difference of intention. As the interpreter of the Concerto in D major only had one hand, the composer is not content simply to make the adjustment : by a remarkable inversion of values he contrasts the unconstrained nimbleness of the Concerto in G major with the tragic vehemence of the Concerto for left hand.

This is one of Ravel's most masterly works, and certainly the most beautiful he had written since the war. Apart from its value as a *tour de force*, this great composition strangely transcends its object, as if manipulating recalcitrant material and outraging nature, demanded of the artist that unknown power which haunts one of his last songs.

The fever and dash of this concerto gives it the force of an incantation. In order to weave new spells it reawakens the fantastic and clandestine inhabitants of *Gaspard de la Nuit*, and even the poetic bestiary of the *Histoires Naturelles*. The orchestra has quite a new sound, alternately heavy and gloomy, and dry and brutal, at moments shot with fiery glimmers and jarred by the syncopation of tortured jazz, which is alternately appeased and opposed by the magical left hand which weaves the most extraordinary arabesques on the piano.[1]

In its compact and perfect form, the Concerto in D major is a complete whole. The strict unity of the composition only makes the nervous character of the work more obvious, flooding the night-world with a weird light and providing the most clear-cut form for flamboyant poetry.

1932 imposed fresh triumphs and fatigues on Maurice Ravel. A few days after the first performance of the Concerto in G major, he left for a grand tour of concerts in Central Europe with Marguerite Long as his interpreter. The same year, at the

---

[1] M. Jacques Février was, and still is, the accepted interpreter of this exacting and devilish virtuoso Concerto.

beginning of October, he was in a taxi which came into collision with another vehicle. He was slightly concussed ; but he had less pain than his friends had fear for him.

At this point a film company chose to make a simultaneous proposal to Manuel de Falla, Ravel, Milhaud, Jacques Ibert and Marcel Delannoy to write film music for " Don Quixote," with Chaliapin as the hero. None of them was, of course, aware that the others had been asked. Ravel, knowing nothing of cinema technique, courageously set to work. We owe to his lack of success the poems of *Don Quichotte à Dulcinée*, on three texts by M. Paul Morand. They are pleasant, semi-typical songs, the second a gentle prayer and the third gaily reminiscent of the Spain of *panderetas* and Gonzalvo's romantic epic.

Je bois à la joie !

But alas ! with the last verse of this bacchanalian refrain and unrestrained toast, Ravel bade a perpetual farewell to music.

All the same he had endless plans ; the eternal *Schéhérazade* of his early youth, Galland's sultaness, once more invaded his dreams ; his first and only love, the harbinger of the fairy kingdom which Colette helped him to discover " in the heart of the rose and the scent of the white lily." He confided to Mme Ida Rubinstein and his close friends, his plan to turn *L'Histoire d'Ali Baba : Morgiane* into a drama, a rich and terrible drama " full of blood and thunder." He managed to outline it, although he found it increasingly difficult to work.

The illness which threatened him began to show itself, if not to reveal its name. About the middle of 1933, he found it inexplicably difficult to write or even to sign his name. An excellent swimmer, he noticed when bathing at Saint-Jean-de-Luz that he was suddenly not able to perform certain movements. Medical advice counselled intellectual relaxation and a mountain holiday. On the 14th March he left for Mt. Pèlerin, near Lausanne. He became more and more worried about it. He seemed to be paralysed by silent forebodings. Certain gestures and words no longer responded to his will.

From the beginning to the very end, we could comfort ourselves that nothing had happened to his perception ; his clear, exacting intelligence was not in any way affected by the deficiencies of its instrument. The doctors whose opinion was

Maurice Ravel in 1935 during a visit to Rhune (Léon Leyritz).

Maurice Ravel in 1935 at Saint-Jean-de-Luz : from left to right, Ravel, M. X, Léon Leyritz (Léon Leyritz).

A typical pose of Ravel
                (Mme. Jourdan-Morhange).

Maurice Ravel on his death bed (Luc-Albert Moreau).

asked murmured the words " apraxia " and " dysphasia," common terms for various cerebral conditions without in any way involving mental derangement. They eventually discarded the possibility of a tumour and arteriosclerosis and admitted that the patient—patient in every sense of the word—was suffering from a congenital illness affecting that part of the brain which is connected with the control of language. The illness, neutralized at first, finally overtook the motor mechanisms which put the conscious mind in touch with the outer world. His extremely alert mind, which up to now had let nothing remain in shadow, felt that shadow little by little surround, if not invade, it. In his own words, he complained of " living in a fog."

His friends busied themselves in taking his mind off it, and contrived distraction for him in the form of travel. His brother and the two faithful Delages took him about everywhere.

Unseen and attentive, with a disarming, secret devotion and inimitable discretion, Mme Rubinstein, without anyone being aware of it, undertook to ease his fate and to arrange wonderful surprises. He regretted his inadequate knowledge of his beloved Spain, the country second in his affections, and he longed to see Morocco ; such a state of affairs was not to be borne ; so on the 15th February, 1935, he left for a wonderful journey, accompanied by Léon Leyritz.

With his exact memory for places and the sense of direction which never forsook him, he guided Leyritz across Madrid and made him visit the little churches forgotten by tourists. They saw the Escorial and embarked at Algeciras for Tangiers. They spent three weeks at Marrakesh. The son of El Glaoui gave an entertainment in their honour. The concert, the dances, and the beauty of El Glaoui's black greyhounds enchanted Ravel and revived his obsession for *Morgiane*.

At Mamounia, before Ravel awoke every morning, Leyritz threw breadcrumbs to attract the birds on the terrace which adjoined his room. Ravel lay in wait for the cry of the muezzin ; but other strains lay in wait for him : at Si Mammri he heard the music of the Moors of Granada and—would you believe it—a Moroccan passing by whistled the *Boléro*.

The tour continued via Kasba-Tadla and Fez, where M. Boris Masslow produced wonders, which, according to the

Director of Fine Arts, were " fit inspiration for him." " If I write something arabic," Ravel answered, " it will be much more arabic than any of that . . ."

On their return journey, the two friends lingered in Andalusia. Leyritz introduced Ravel to Seville and in exchange was promised a visit to Cordova. At Seville, they met Ernesto Halffter. An evening at the Variedades gave Ravel his first direct experience of the real *cante jondo* and its famous interpreter, *Niña de los peines*. The *cantaora* loved to keep her audience in a state of expectancy—all the more reason for Ravel to admire her. At Cordova, Ravel this time was the one who lingered. After a while they left without having seen the Mosque . . .

In August of the same year (1935) Léon Leyritz joined him at Saint-Jean-de-Luz. Together they left for the Cantabrian coast, Bilbao and Burgos, and returned via Pamplona and Roncesvalles.

He enjoyed these journeyings. But, alas, they did not hinder the relentless development of his illness. As clear-headed and patient as ever, Ravel felt the mist thickening round him. He avoided being alone as much as he could and right to the end was able to smile at his relations and friends. He could be met more often at concerts and theatres than in the days when he wrote the works which were performed there. Were it not for the shadow of sadness which occasionally darkened his face, no change was discernible in his charming and silent courtesy.

From now on his time was divided between Montfort, his brother's house at Levallois, and that of Maurice Delage. Manuel Rosenthal used to spend much time with him. Lucien Garban took care of his correspondence and musical business. He could often be found with Mme Marguerite Long and M. and Mme Jacques Meyer, who took him to Le Touquet.

But every day the pain got worse. The summer of 1937, which he spent at the " Belvédère," was terribly trying in spite of the devotion of his faithful housekeeper, Mme Révelot, who was in his service for nearly fifteen years.

The perturbing symptoms increased during the autumn. In despair as to the cause, it was decided to risk a major operation. It took place on the 19th December, 1937, at the nursing-home in the Rue Boileau. I can still see Ravel, heroic to the bitter end, with a turban of white bandages, on the evening before the operation, laughing at the unsuspected likeness we thought he showed to Lawrence of Arabia.

The operation left him in a state of semi-consciousness which lasted a whole week. On Monday the 27th his life drew quietly to its end and he died without suffering in the small hours of the 28th December.

Maurice Ravel's death was deeply mourned by the whole musical world. And it was immediately apparent that the disappearance of one of the greatest composers of our time was felt no less acutely in other countries outside France—England, Germany and the U.S.A. in particular. For it is common knowledge that France reckons music of little importance among the diverse occupations of her citizens. So that it only intensified one's emotion to read, among obituary eulogies, not infrequently of doubtful accuracy,[1] some accounts in which praise and regret were sincerely mixed.

" With Maurice Ravel," wrote Emile Vuillermoz, " disappeared the greatest French composer of our time. After the death of Gabriel Fauré and Claude Debussy, the torch of our national art has until now burnt brightly in his hands . . . He towered over all the musicians of his time . . ."

It is often stated that some of the most fitting of the tributes to which I refer were made by composers of a generation represented, rightly or wrongly, as being hostile to Ravel.

" At the beginning of the twentieth century," wrote Georges Auric in *Paris-Soir*, " Maurice Ravel, together with Claude Debussy, embodied an outlook by turns exquisitely finished and emotionally moving. But though he was exquisite, he never became affected or precious, and right to the end he used to move us by the most effortless expression."

" France," declared Darius Milhaud, " has lost one of her most distinguished composers . . . the astonishing perfection of his technique, and the certainty with which his work was

---

[1] An odd enough example of inaccuracy is that of an article published by an important Parisian journal, on the 4th January, 1938, bearing Maurice Ravel's signature : *Mes souvenirs d'enfant paresseux* (Reminiscences of a lazy childhood). M. Edouard Ravel has allowed me to express grave doubt about the authenticity of a document whose manner and style reveal another hand, and whose original no one has been able to produce.

carried out, make him one of the most faultless masters of our day . . ."

In *Candide*, Henri Sauguet recalled the obligations of " countless generations . . . even those who appeared to scorn him. At a time when it was correct to react against what was called impressionism, Ravel's music suffered attacks from the musicians of the time. Once their work was on a sure footing, they quickly realized the greatness of his music, which, as one of its most distinguishing characteristics, bore live witness to French genius."

The funeral took place on Thursday, 30th December, 1937, attended by a great crowd of friends, known and unknown. Igor Stravinsky rubbed shoulders with obscure admirers and young musicians attached to Ravel through gratitude, who had become his friends through the kindliness with which he had received them.

During the interment, a funeral oration was delivered by the Minister of Education, representing the Government :

". . . If I call to mind," said M. Jean Zay, " the greatest names in our moral and artistic tradition . . . I am led to ask myself what is the common factor in all this genius, and what is essential to Ravel's genius ; I think I have found it throughout to be a supremely intelligent capacity to contemplate phenomena, however passionate or moving, and to submit such phenomena to the discipline of a style. No power of emotion is excluded from the French tradition. When we submit we do not go under . . ."

Maurice Ravel is buried in the cemetery at Levallois, beside the parents to whom he had been so devoted.

PART TWO

CHAPTER XII

The formation of Ravel's style—his three periods—stylistic elements : melody, harmony, instrumental and vocal writing—the motivating forces : Spain and the Dance, Comedy and Magic.

THE FIRST THING TO STRIKE US IF WE TAKE A COMPREHENSIVE view of Ravel's work is the unity of design in its development. He was a born musician, destined for music from his earliest childhood, and so naturally adapted for the task set him by his father and masters, that the problem of a vocation was quickly solved for him.

Work which matures under such conditions will not, at least at the outset, bear marks of a romantic conflict between temperament and destiny. Ravel made music as easily as an apple-tree grows apples. But the difficulties spared him by life and denied him by nature he felt bound to create for himself artificially. For his academic experience soon showed him that a sure foundation can only be built on some resisting material ; the appeal of a technique implies and demands the severity of rules.

Such a craftsman does not distinguish between the effects of his own industry and the products of nature. He believes, like a child, that the first are as simple as the second. It is well known how Ravel, then a pupil at the Conservatoire, commented one day to his friend M.-D. Calvocoressi on the opinion of the people who taxed him with affectation : " Does it never dawn on these people that I may be artificial by nature ? " [1]

Man, in so far as he is creative, creates out of his subconscious. He has to grapple with recalcitrant material, and to exhaust his facile gifts against some technical obstacle. The only function of hindrances, restraining forces and the refined forms of difficulty are to allow the artist to acquire and develop the only quality which springs from his diligence—his style.

[1] Quoted by M.-D. Calvocoressi in *Music and Ballet*, London. Faber and Faber, 1933, p. 51.

Thus from the arbitrary Ravel made straight for the inevitable, to use Valéry's terms. The evolution of his genius led him uncompromisingly from the complex to the simple ; the direction of his effort is evident in this continuity of development.

Ravel's true style was formed very soon. The *Habañera* of 1895 proves that much. There he stabilizes that style with a brilliance and conciseness which found no counterpart in the works of the same period : for the work was an anticipation.

About 1900, the composer was less sure of himself. He underwent some restraining influence. The genius of Claude Debussy, so remote and yet so close, crossed his path too often to allow him to progress with unruffled assurance. But the disturbance was brief ; the nostalgic lyricism of *Schéhérazade* and the transports of enthusiasm in the Quartet might well show a slight trace of Debussy's influence, but nothing of its constraint.

The *Miroirs*, composed in 1905, mark the beginning of what rightly could be called (allowing for the arbitrary nature of all such divisions) Ravel's second period. This year 1905 and the year following his final rebuff at the " Concours de Rome," were happy ones in which he felt both unentangled and alert, and which proved that his powers responded effortlessly to his will.

The common characteristics of the works of this period (*Miroirs, Histoires Naturelles, Rapsodie Espagnole, L'Heure Espagnole, Gaspard de la Nuit, Daphnis et Chloé*) were flexibility of form within the structural outline ; richness and magnificence in the basic harmonies in keeping with the exacting caprices of a smooth and compact melodic line.

But the modest intentions of *Ma Mère l'Oye* had immense consequences ; it stayed the torrential overflow of harmonies and with childlike grace rediscovered most opportunely the importance of melody. So that the vast display of virtuosity which abounds in *Gaspard de la Nuit* are substituted in the *Valses Nobles et Sentimentales* for the telling clarity of the writing which " condenses the harmony and brings out the contrasts," to use the composer's phrase. These hard chords, closed in as it were upon themselves and capable of detaching themselves at will, remove from the tonality the danger of shifting harmonies in which the character of dissonances is weakened.

They also free the melody and guide the musician to a more strictly organic statement.

The *Valses Nobles et Sentimentales* come as a " milestone," according to M. Mantelli, on the triumphal progress of Ravel's art. The essential elements of his arrangement of chords are condensed in this unique work. Ravel makes it a kind of reservoir on which he was often to draw for his subsequent works.

This control of the harmonic appetite to the advantage of the melody is pursued differently, but significantly, in the quintessential music distilled in the *Trois Poèmes de Stéphane Mallarmé* and the Trio, whose austerity is both passionate and chaste.

The second period, so rich in " masterpieces " (a word Ravel did not like) emphasizes his continual effort to clarify the writing and improve the melodic line.

The third and last period, beginning with *La Valse* of 1920, gradually brings the process of rejection to a climax, sometimes in a spirit of feverish fury, contrasting with the spiritual serenity dominating the earlier period. The perorations of *La Valse*, the Duo-Sonata, *Boléro* and the Concerto for left hand alone, take on an anguished and almost terrified character in which now there blows the tempest, now the dying gasp of a lost soul, as though the final notes of these works bade music a pathetic and despairing farewell.

But the *Chansons Madécasses*, *Ronsard à son âme*, and the second half of *L'Enfant et les Sortilèges* preserve, with lovable simplicity, a pure and fervent lyricism that smiles through tears and offers, at the last limit of tension and aridity, a touching message of tenderness.

Among the fundamentals of Ravel's style, melody must obviously be considered first.

A series of sounds in which the idea of interval is forgotten, [1] melody is the mysterious essence of music. Mysterious, because it is the rarest of gifts, and without it all the hard work and application of mere skill are of no value. Continuity of the line, charm of the phrase, clarity of design, in short the movement of the melody and its unity in diversity, reveal the profound genius of a composer, just as his inner weakness is betrayed by the padding and reiterating of a theme. Rhythm controls this activity.

[1] M. Arthur Lourié's definition.

The fate of melody is inevitably bound up with the changing view of musicians about tonality. Whether we admit it or not, all European melody implies the diatonic. Ravel never forgets it ; and not the least of his claims to fame will be to have recalled music to a respect for this fundamental principle, while retaining all his love of innovation and fantasy within the limits of tonality.

The modern French school, following Emmanuel Chabrier (and differing from the German school), has generally refused to limit tonality to the dual system of major and minor. Ravel's melodies are definitely *modal*. They fall as naturally into the ancient modes as the old folk-songs of the French provinces. The fact is patent. What is infinitely more remarkable is that in Ravel the practice is quite unconscious. The harmony he learnt at the Conservatoire, which was adequate for him all his life, postulates the absolute value of the scale of C, formed by a group of two similar tetrachords and artificially altered to form a minor scale.

Ravel had never been initiated into the modal theory, like Saint-Saëns, Messager, Fauré and the pupils of the Niedermeyer School. Irrevocably loyal to Reber and Dubois and completely indifferent to the study of ancient modes, he had nevertheless from his earliest youth subjected melodies in a pure Dorian mode to the laws of a system of harmony which did not recognize their existence.

For with Ravel the major is only one of the many modes, and he seldom uses it without preventing the leading-note from yielding to the attraction of the tonic. As for the classic minor, I have not found a single characteristic example.

Ravel's use of melody most frequently falls into the Dorian and Phrygian modes with a marked preference for the first.[1]

The first mode is mediæval *par excellence*. Ravel found many examples in old French folk-songs, and even more in Chabrier, the composer from Auvergne (*Le Roi malgré Lui*) and the Russian Moussorgsky. It is also interesting to note that, according to Father Donostia, this mode is characteristic of Basque music, a peculiarity which distinguishes it from the

---

[1] The reader unfamiliar with this nomenclature will forgive the unavoidable pedantry of the exposition. In the main he can get an idea of the Dorian and Phrygian modes by playing on the white keys of a piano the two scales whose tonics are respectively D and E.

rest of Spanish music. Countless examples of it point to Ravel's use of a " gapped " scale :

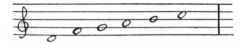

In this framework Ravel's favourite melodic formulæ appear. To facilitate illustration I have transposed most of the examples:

Menuet antique

Lors que je voy en or-dre la bru-net-te

D'Anne jouant de l'Espinette

Daphnis et Chloé

Sonate en duo

Concerto en sol

The Phrygian mode, typical of ancient music, is also essentially characteristic of the Spanish provincial songs, and particularly of the Andalusian *Cante Flamenco*. From the moment his muse travels " tras los montes," Ravel's music instinctively adopts this mode.

L'*Heure Espagnole* can provide many more examples of borrowing from this mode in Ravel's music under Spanish influence. *Boléro*, however, is an exception to the rule. Equally important is the use of the same mode in the magnificent opening phrase of *Soupir*, the first of the *Trois Poèmes de Stéphane Mallarmé*.

Along with the profound attraction of these two modes there sometimes comes the memory of the ' gapped ' scales of the Far East, which were for so long the delight of the very young visitor to the 1889 Exhibition.

The spirited *chinoiserie* of *Laideronnette, Impératrice des Pagodes*, will naturally make use of the same scale.

It goes without saying that Ravel did not confine himself indefinitely within the narrow framework of the same mode ; especially as he considered that tonality is the focal point towards which every development in the melody converges, and it is instinct alone which makes him pile up his modal modulations, so much more natural in that they are not expected of him.

The particular character of the Ravelian *melos* can be

seen in a system of chords which often seems to be a projection of melody into the harmonic plan ; the origin of the chords is in the arpeggio ; the horizontal is made up of the vertical.

From this arises the marked preference in his harmony for the chords known as secondary sevenths and ninths, which are naturally formed on modal tonics of D and E :

The very frequent use of the second of these chords brings Ravel into line with Puccini in an unsuspected but unmistakable way, as Casella has pointed out. They are chords which form the harmonic foundation of Ravel's first period compositions. They acquire relief and enrichment from internal pedals, appoggiaturas and constant acciaccaturas.

The *Miroirs* acquire another fresh enchantment which is used with significant persistence : to use academic language, again, it is an unresolved changing note at the seventh in the chord of the diminished seventh :

This chord becomes increasingly important in the works of the second period and flashes out with its greatest brilliance in the *Valses Nobles et Sentimentales*, continually sharpening the sweep of the phrases :

The *Valses Nobles et Sentimentales* form the climax of Ravel's harmonic experience. All discords are left bare ; their harsh gaiety will never be surpassed. The work appeared at a time when French music, in the flush of its first triumph and the pride of a supremacy which the world was beginning to acknowledge, had come to a turning point in its history. It had discovered among its ancestral documents a dangerous axiom, which it put into practice a little too freely : " Our guide is harmony," said Jean-Philippe Rameau. When the *Valses* appeared in 1911, the harmonic innovations current among the young French musicians were excessive. It was a dangerous armaments race, which was to lead to a new war of harmony and counterpoint whose issue is still undecided.

The two finest craftsmen in the French musical hegemony seem to have estimated the danger fairly accurately. They were the first to raise the standard against the attacks sometimes made in their name against the sovereignty of the tonal principle. It was not enough for Debussy to hope that music would be " de-congested " ; indeed, from the time of his orchestral *Images* he did not cease striving in that direction. And Ravel's experiments were even more decisive and uncompromising.

In general, their means of expression differ as much as their temperaments. It has been rightly pointed out that Debussy's harmony is distinguished by chords of the major ninth, and Ravel's by secondary ninths. The use they each make of the famous chord of the augmented fifth is also sufficient proof of their differing techniques. There is no instance where this chord has involved the smallest suspicion of a whole-tone scale in Ravel. As for the tritone, *diabolus in musica*, Debussy alone, guided and upheld by his genius, descended to the Magic Chamber scene of the Witches of d'Annunzio without losing his footing. But his imitators have lost the sense of tonality just as fatally as did the slaves of chromatic polyphony on the Wagnerian and Franckist slipways.

The chord of the augmented fifth in Ravel is an integral part of the chord of the natural eleventh :

as, for example, *Le Grillon* (the Cricket) in the *Histoires Naturelles*, where the augmented fifth is first heard separately and then startles us by revealing its origin.

Ravel loved saying that there was no such thing as well-orchestrated music—only well-written music. And, indeed, everyone who has tried to extract the secret of his orchestral spell has regularly been defeated in the attempt. Consider, in particular, the orchestral score of the *Tombeau de Couperin*. Although it is a transcription of a work originally intended for piano, the orchestra never appears to be an added finery, but rather a strict adjustment of a series of sounds to the polyphonic ensemble. *Boléro* itself, the famous *Boléro*, that " merry-go-round of tone-colours," where the composer seems to rely on the powers of the orchestra to vary the invariable, only aims after all at giving balance and proportion to a network of sound of increasing intensity : " In these successful fabrications, nothing appears unless it serves a purpose : nothing is kept unless it springs uniquely from whatever is necessary to produce the effect." [1]

This does not mean that Ravel in his early work did not make small concessions to picturesque orchestration : *Schéhérazade*, in 1903, gave its hearers a most wonderfully ingenious mosaic of sound. But Ravel quickly exhausted the pleasures and difficulties of such versatile antics. Granted that he admired Rimsky-Korsakov, who in this was his first model, for the astonishing adaptability of his instruments to their appointed functions, he very quickly realized that the apparent miracle was only sleight of hand ; that so admirable a balance could hardly ever be obtained without prejudicing the quality of the music. It is not the instrument which adapts itself to the caprices of the phrases, but the phrases which yield to tyranny of the instrument. In the *Russian Easter Festival* Overture, " that incredible piece without any music in it," Ravel used to say—and in the *Capriccio Espagnol* the orchestral virtuosity becomes an end in itself, as the composer himself admitted. In the *Rapsodie Espagnole* it is only a means but it is no less indebted to Rimsky—and to Richard Strauss—for some part of its brilliance. A means : but so strictly related to its end that it is easily confused with it, as has actually happened.

[1] Paul Valéry : *Eupalinos*.

117

Here, again, Ravel differs from Debussy. Ravel's orchestration, under the influence of Verlaine, demands that

> . . . *la nuance seule fiance*
> *Le rêve au rêve et la flûte au cor.* [1]

Anxious to ally or juxtapose sonorities obviously not intended for each other, Debussy's orchestration, under the influence of Baudelaire, appears to maintain that expression depends on the shades of meaning, and intensity on the timbre, range and number of instruments. This perhaps explains why Ravel, differing from Debussy, expects virtuosity from the instrumentalists, rather than initiative from the conductor.

In Ravel, the shades of meaning generally arise from the strength of an instrument in a given tessitura : to force which would be useless. On the other hand, he has a fondness for extreme registers (his oboes and bassoons in sharp keys—his clarinets in flat ones). Sometimes they involve perilous but indispensable acrobatics.

" Debussy's writing," writes M. Vuillermoz, " calls for the co-operation of an active sensibility. Ravel only asks for a respectful attention . . . There are many ways of playing Debussy. There is only one way to play Ravel." [2]

Liszt's immediate successors hardly questioned his heritage. Except for Saint-Saëns, they were not anxious so much to give the piano new resources as to use it as a confidant or accomplice in their effusions, and they ceased to serve it as virtuosi in order to subject it to vague caprices of feeling.

A personal confession from Ravel's keyboard is not to be expected. The composer of *Jeux d'Eau* takes up, extends and surpasses Liszt's experiments, giving them something of the light and fluent clarity of a spiritual son of Domenico Scarlatti. It is pleasant to come across M. Henri Gil-Marchex, who in a study of rare insight sees exactly the relationship between the Basque and the Spanish-Neapolitan composer : the same skill in the finger mechanisms, the constant use of

---

[1] From Verlaine's *Art Poétique.*
    " The shade of meaning alone links dream to dream, the flute to the horn."

[2] *Le style orchestral.* Number of the *Revue Musicale* devoted to Maurice Ravel 1st April, 1925.

thumb passages " frequently combined with repeated notes. The use of the thumb is very remarkable in Ravel's piano work. The thumb takes control—especially in *Gaspard de la Nuit*, which contains some of the most characteristic discoveries of his supreme technique."

" . . . he was content—for he never practised," continues M. Gil-Marchex, " to be a fairly good pianist whose hands were possibly the tyrants of musical creation, as Weber wrote of himself. He sat incredibly low at the piano and this peculiarity may perhaps be the reason why he never used octave passages ; the long and agile fingers, the slender hand joined to an extremely supple wrist seemed to be those of a conjuror ; he could twist his thumb into the palm of the hand with unbelievable facility which allowed him without any trouble to press down three keys at a time. This thumb explains the passages in seconds in *Scarbo*."[1]

Vocal writing falls naturally into line with the general trend of Ravel's style and should adequately show stages in his evolution.

It is in this part of his work that inevitably and in the clearest possible manner there appear successive phases of the patient conquest which led the composer from the deliberately uniform pointing of *Un grand Sommeil Noir* and *Sainte* to the empassioned cantilena of *L'Enfant* and the *Chansons madécasses*. Even in the *Deux épigrammes de Marot* (1898) his desire to treat the vocal line as a real part of the ensemble is made evident, which, according to M. Guido Pannain, is a distinctive characteristic of the *declamato* of Ravel.[2]

Ravel's second manner corresponds to his successful discovery of a personal kind of lyrical declamation, which pursues the most fleeting inflexions of the spoken language without prejudicing the metrical diversity demanded by the melody. The prose of the *Histoires Naturelles* entices Ravel to use his talents on literary material which is exceedingly dry and inappropriate to lyrical treatment. The success of *Le Paon* should have assured him that he was now the master of a type of melodic recitative peculiarly his own.

[1] *La technique de piano :* previously quoted number of *La Revue Musicale*.
[2] " Maurice Ravel " ; in *Rassenga musicale*. Turin, 1928, No. 1.

Les vo-lailles ha-bi-tuées ne lè-vent même point la

tê-te Elles sont lasses de l'ad-mi - rer Il re-des

cend dans la cour si sûr d'être beau- qu'il est in-ca-pable de ran-cu-ne

L'Heure Espagnole, a musical conversation, follows the same procedure. The language of the music is linked up as naturally as possible with the music of the language : an achievement without parallel in French Comic-Opera. This multiform and peculiar prosody faithfully follows normal speech. " More often than not," as M. Arthur Hoerée has so well said, " his melodic phrase is simply a reproduction of the declamatory sound-pattern. This declamatory style slips in between the rise and fall of cæsura and rhymes, an infinite variety of metres linked to the secondary accents of the alexandrine, surpassing the most rhythmical versification in richness. Sometimes the inflexions of his phrases give the wrong emphasis to the weak beats ; sometimes the declamation tactfully elides an inopportune mute syllable, so strictly does it guard its own supple naturalness . . ." [1] Continuing to follow rhythm and intonation of the words extremely accurately, it reveals melody. A unique *tour de force* in a language which is, by nature, the least accentuated and the least singable that can be imagined.

But the *Trois Poèmes de Stéphane Mallarmé* look elsewhere for the discipline of perfection. The rhythm of the *mélos*, approximating to the regularity of metre, depends less on contrast than on continuity of design. The declamation here becomes less strict but gains in pure music what it loses in accuracy.

The vocal technique of Ravel's final period exploits this tendency to the full. In this respect *L'Enfant et les Sortilèges* and the *Chansons madécasses* are significant. Interest in the

---

[1] *Les mélodies et l'œuvre vocale :* previously quoted number of *La Revue Musicale*.

Ravel conducting his *Boléro*. (Sketch by Croquis de Luc-Albert Moreau).

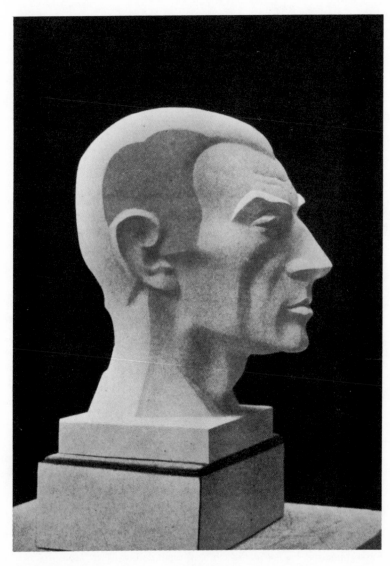

A bust of Maurice Ravel by Leon Leyritz.

melodic line, a concrete entity, takes complete precedence over the exigencies of the spoken word.

In order to affirm his affinity with the ancient tradition of dramatic music, Ravel puts the scene of the Princess in the heart of the action in *L'Enfant et les Sortilèges*, making that love-duet one of the great successes in the score. In it every law of the genre is observed and every one of its characteristics appear, except indiscretion . . . No longer is it a musical conversation, but a simple discussion turned into music, an *arioso* recitative which turns into an air in the central section of a *lied*. The expression broadens to the point of lyricism in the course of a large section whose eloquence is no longer surprising : melody has ceased to be the slave of the word and has become a companion free to develop according to its own nature.

Ravel wrote relatively little for chorus. The vocal ensembles of *Daphnis et Chloé* have a purely decorative function in a score where they seem to be superimposed—with the exception of an interlude dominated by a somewhat unexpected chromaticism.

The only choral works to invite comment would be the three delightful songs for mixed chorus which he both wrote and composed, were it not for the magnificent peroration of *L'Enfant et les Sortilèges*, also intended for unaccompanied chorus, in which a fugal style is used with splendid freshness, serenity and fullness.

This ode to kindness gives the work profound significance. It ennobles it ; it so enhances it that the last page of the score is one of the composer's most beautiful and most harmonious. Music of the spirit and sensibility, filled with tenderness. Emotion born in the heart of trees and birds and all the little people of the night, which dies with a sob on the threshold of the house of man.

I shall not consider as sources of Ravel's inspiration the literary stimuli of his work—which have already been closely studied by M. René Chalupt.[1] I prefer to look at the favourite themes which dominate his work : Spain, first, and then the Dance—the former so often bound up in the latter. Finally, in a more general sense, comedy and enchantment—the only

---

[1] *M.R. et les prétextes littéraires de sa musique* : *Revue Musicale*, number previously quoted.

subjects of his dramatic work and of practically all his programme-music, if any of it has a programme.

" The art of Gipsy music," wrote the admirable Valencian musicologist Eduardo López Chavarri, " has inspired moderns such as Stravinsky, Debussy and Ravel, who, when they write works of Spanish character, do not claim to make music in the Spanish style, like Bizet, but in the Spanish tongue, or, more correctly, in the tongue of Andalusia." [1] In Ravel's case the assertion cannot be denied. It does not need mentioning in connection with a Basque for whom Spain is another homeland, and for whom the Pyrenees do not exist. Let us say straight away that in the Spanish hostelries and watch-makers' shops Ravel found much more than he brought with him. What is more, with amused complacence he has given the finest possible ear to every " sound of the Caleta "—and to every so-called Spanish refrain. And he has made us share his delight and enjoyment of the flavour of the true through the spiciness of the fictitious.

He confessed himself to be attracted to a certain type of Spanish music shamelessly derived from the Italian, a tradition which lasted throughout the nineteenth century to emerge as the *zarzuela*. Amused and delighted by what he himself called " the Louis-Philippe *habañeras*," he abandoned a false Andalusia to conquer a Spain which, though not genuine, seems to be more convincing than the real Spain, because its creator has known how to give it the semblance of the natural and necessary : " Nature is free as air," says Chesterton somewhere, " but art is forced to give the semblance of probability." Thus the French Ravel created a virtue out of *flamenquisme*, which according to his friend Manuel de Falla, is the vice common to Spanish composers.

This virtue enlivens the *habañeras*, *malagueñas*, and *boléros* which crowd his work, and especially the best pages of *L'Heure Espagnole* : for instance Gonzalve's arietta, in the form of a *malagueña*, and, even more, the final quintet, which is a bravura *habañera*, with passages enlivened by trills and staccato arpeggios. In this brilliant work, the singers are alternately opposed and identified with an orchestra of soloists, who at their most brilliant retain enough clarity never to drown the voices, and

[1] *Musica popular española*, Ed. Labor, Barcelona, 1927, p. 147.

enough preciseness to allow a 6/8 to run with impunity alongside the imperturbable 2/4 of the *habañera*. The enchantment of this firework display is so irresistible that it drew from M. Pierre Lalo in 1922 sincere enthusiasm and loyal praise : ". . . a rich and delightful bouquet of every kind of flower . . . the product of so consummate an art as to remind the hearer of those pieces of supreme virtuosity, those masterpieces by which, in crafts of past ages, a composer used to acquire mastery, and which remained an example to future craftsmen." —(*Le Temps*, 3rd February, 1922).

Ravel was so attracted to Spain that he sometimes took to composing in the Spanish manner during the course of a page of pure music when his subject did not demand it ; for instance, in the *pantoum* of his Trio. The first movement of this Trio is a curious example of his carefree disposition. The composer admits, in his own words, that the first theme of the piece has a " basque flavour." But neither the style nor the mode of this theme justifies the assertion. And when in all good faith he thinks he is expressing himself in the Basque idiom, then pure Castillian appears.

The lost *Cancionero* of Olmeda [1] provides a curious specimen of *bailo a lo llano* which is analogous with Ravel's theme. For the *bailo a lo llano* is the primitive form of the Castillian *fandango* which could have been heard by Ravel in the market-place of Saint-Jean-de-Luz ; a curious local melody which has crossed the mountains.

" The dance," wrote M. André Suarès, " influences all Ravel's music, just as it does that of the Spaniards and the clavecinists." To the Basque Ravel the supremacy of the dance was as much the result of a natural inclination as a conscious intention to give formal structure to his creations.

Minuets, pavanes, passacaglias, the forlane, the rigaudon, every variety of waltz, *czarda*, *habañera*, *boléro*, fox-trot and " blues " : Ravel delighted to borrow their steps and multiply them in his work, but he never forgot that the symphony, the sonata, and the various forms of chamber-music were the perverted daughters of the *Suite*, which, to use the significant word of the old clavecinists, is itself an *Order* of dances.

[1] Frederico Olmeda. *Folklore de Burgos*, Burgos, 1902.

In epochs when music tended to express emotion, it was naturally eager to extend its frontiers—and even to destroy them. Ravel took timely note of Verdi's advice ; he went back to the old to discover the new. His love of the dance gave him the opportunity to condense the strict forms still further, and to give the tension he imposed on them a source of energy and the secret of lightness.

A consideration of Ravel's favourite subjects leads us to notice that they inevitably depend either on comedy or on " Faerie," or else on the two together. The vehemence of tragedy is consistently a forbidden subject, doubtless because before it enslaves the masses, it tries to enslave the dramatist, and Ravel, determined to master his subject, could not allow himself to be dominated by it. He knew, or guessed, that if tragedy is recognized as the acknowledged dupe of the passions it aroused, then it is the function of comedy to judge those passions, and of " Faerie " to free them from human bondage. Thus Ravel's dramatic work gives us images of life which some-times mock and parody, and which are sometimes ennobled by strange contrivances.

Much has been criticized in an æsthetic system which, in Nietzsche's words, never stirs up the mud, nor enriches the world of passions, and only approaches the human by way of analogy. It cannot be denied, to take one example, that the same arrangement which in *L'Heure Espagnole* serves to describe the amorous aspirations of an aged gallant, is used again for the apparition of the " chien sombre " in the *Noël des Jouets* and is found practically note for note in *Ma Mère l'Oye*, where it represents the Beast repulsed by Beauty.

When a man like Ravel makes use of the study of an animal to describe a lascivious dotard rendered positively terrifying by the grotesque spectacle of his desire ; or when a man like Stravinsky models the activities of the negro in *Pétrouchka* on the antics of a wild animal in a cage, all either of them does is to find the " phantasm "—or the most representative musical image for the particular form or idea. They determine the symbol which changes into stable objects, and catch the secret movement of impenetrable hearts, the mystery of featureless things.

Such a conception of art, surely the most likely to allow of the penetration of poetry by reason, corresponds to the classical system of æsthetics. Where Ravel is concerned, his particular type of temperamental make-up in some strange way sustains him in such a conception.

This is the great mystery of Ravel, the secret power which gives the calculated graces of his art an angelic charm which is at its freest in the world of the supernatural. It is the secret of a profound sensibility which could not freely relax or feel profoundly except in the world of the inhuman, or in a world of humanity so spiritualized and idealized as to be preserved from the violence of instincts which from the *Iliad* to tragicomedy, and from *Orfeo* to *La Bohème*, deliver up the heroes of epic and drama to the frenzies of desire and despair.

Mythology opens up to him the gates of grandeur. This is apparent in the nocturne in *Daphnis et Chloé* where, to evoke the marble nymphs who come to life through the power of the magic flame burning in their foreheads, the music first takes us to the Upper Air they breathe and lets us hear that soft and vibrating chord which suggests the harmony of the spheres and the voice of " the night which reveals the night."

Another example is the final scene in the same work, where to begin with, the daybreak is nothing but a mist of arpeggios full of the freshness of the dawn. A few bird-calls escape from the forest of chords. They are echoed by the pipe of the shepherd-boy. Then a melody gushes up from the depths of the orchestra, which is the song of dawn itself. And in this we have the most beautiful emotional confession ever to come from Ravel, the most generous confidence to escape from a heart so careful of its secrets as in the end to express only the most magnificent. In it the sensualist is carried far beyond his dreams and looks down from above upon the house of Aristippus and the garden of Epicurus. Here, at the very limit of effort and calculation, he attains that true and measureless greatness, that pure beauty which is at one with the apparent simplicity of nature, reconciling reason and passion for a moment in supreme lyricism.

Ravel was master of an enchanted world, peopled by children, gods, fairies, compassionate animals, turbulent puppets, clockmakers without souls and immortal clocks : a kingdom fit for Ariel—or for Vaucanson. Those characters without the rigidity of automata are agile and subtle, impenetrable and clear like celestial forms.

What magic controls the charms of Ariel and the devices of Vaucanson in this " green paradise of childish loves " ?   That is the triumph of his technique, and the secret of his genius. From it springs the triumph of *classicism*, which sets out merely to present the real through the play of conventions and rules, but which, having started from a vision of actuality, finds an echo in the world of the spirit.

Maurice Ravel in his study at Montfort-l'Amaury in 1933 (Lipnitzki).

CHAPTER XIII

The man—a physical portrait—his character and tastes—the child—the dandy—the craftsman—conclusion.

TO SEE MAURICE RAVEL FOR THE FIRST TIME WAS TO BE surprised at his diminutive height. After a short while it was no longer noticeable, presumably because his hard, spare, agile and slender body was so well proportioned that he appeared in perfect symmetry on a small scale.

After favouring side-whiskers in his youth, he enjoyed allowing his moustache to grow, and trimming his beard, first to a point and later square. In 1910 he threw off the mask and became entirely clean-shaven, at last revealing his real features which were those of a Basque from the coast, with the dark complexion, hollow cheeks, and the long nose common to the daring as well as the naïve type, brilliant, dark, and closely-set eyes, and thin lips, closed as if to hold back a secret. Bushy eyebrows ; black hair, slightly curly, which began to grow grey after the forties, and became white and wavy after 1930. His whole appearance was both gay and enquiring, alert and smiling, the open frankness of his eyes giving the lie to the reserve of the firmly shut lips.

His slender and active hands were admirable for either pianist or conjurer, with their spare fingers and unusually curved thumb. His carriage was light and easy, and remained youthful in spite of the years. His lengthy stride betrayed his double mountain ancestry. His somewhat sombre and " nasal " voice was inclined to be deep. If he ever had occasion to use his singing voice—which only happened under professional pressure—it still showed this so-called *blanche* delivery characteristic of the composer's spoken voice.

Ravel expressed himself very simply with the same spontaneous grace which appears in his letters. He spoke without any particular accent, like a well-bred Parisian. One single linguistic peculiarity betrayed his southern provincial origin ; he constantly forgot to use " si " as an affirmative particle, and used " oui " when he wanted to contradict someone else's affirmation.

He never had the occasion nor perhaps the inclination to exercise and train his natural agility and physical skill. He was content to be an excellent swimmer and a tireless walker. His manual dexterity was very unequal : he was wonderful at modelling small objects with pieces of bread, but he performed the simplest actions clumsily and almost lazily. Here as elsewhere, he was alert and quick in difficult tasks only.

He was extremely fastidious about his appearance, and very obviously attentive to his dress, his ties, the cut of his clothes and the changes in fashion, an absorption which took the form of a most sober elegance which seemed to be unpremeditated.

A confirmed smoker, his " caporal " tobacco was a more tyrannical urge than eating or drinking. It was rare for him to listen to a concert from beginning to end without sacrificing one or more pieces of the programme for a cigarette. It was owing to the remorse which sometimes followed such disappearances that Manuel Rosenthal became his pupil and one of his best friends. At one of the concerts of the *Société musicale indépendante*, which were mostly devoted to performances of works by unknown composers, Ravel slipped away during the playing of a Sonatina for two violins, to smoke what Léon-Paul Fargue used to call " a life-saving cigarette." When he came back we whispered to him that he had missed hearing a remarkable work. Like a child caught doing wrong, the master of *Daphnis et Chloé* went along to introduce himself to Manuel Rosenthal and to make his apologies, and invited him to come and see him. So began a great friendship.

Ravel's appetite was as sound as his digestion and in keeping with the general excellence of his health, which did not deteriorate till the end of his life. A healthy and discriminating eater, without overdoing his interest in food, he was yet the easiest of guests to satisfy when he used to come and take pot-luck. But offer him a good table and he was immediately the more inclined to be critical of it. His race showed itself in a liking for strong wines and spices which he himself called " incendiaries." In the ordinary way, however, he was very moderate in his tastes.

At a first meeting Ravel was courteous and reserved. His

best friends could not help feeling secretly disappointed by the feeling that they were not able to become more fully intimate with him ; for the most devoted sympathy and close relationship scarcely altered the manner of his greeting. It took a long time to discover that Ravel was the surest, most faithful and most profoundly affectionate of friends.

But the sort of affection he gave was virtually incapable of external expression, and only showed itself in unexpected acts and attentions. It seemed as if he felt uncontrollably awkward and almost physically incapable of putting his emotions into words. In short, he was a most sociable person—but the least communicative.

His desire for company, which was one of his fundamental needs, was only equalled by his horror of appearing as the famous man, of being exposed to the curiosity of worldlings and snobs, and having to attempt heartiness with men of position, who inevitably took little time in finding him out as a natural enemy of the Best People.

Ravel was, besides, incapable of adjusting his manners to the social rank of the person talking to him. Unskilled as he was in the art of being nobly bored, he would not have hesitated to turn his back on an Excellency in order to go off and play, like the child he was, with the children of the household.

For Ravel had never left the " green paradise of childhood affections." Genius for him was not Baudelaire's rediscovered childhood, but a childhood which was conserved, ennobled and communicated. At once both objective and credulous in outlook, nothing ever tarnished his pure and simple attitude to the world. The violence of passion and the tyranny of primitive instincts never obscured for him that ingenuous disinterestedness which assures the artist his freedom and guides him without swerving to the fundamental nature of things, leaving him free to absorb whatever he will.

Unlike those contemporary extremists of sincerity who get hold of the wrong end of the stick by being childish in their technique and cunning in spirit, Ravel instead uses cunning in his technique and keeps his spirit childlike. [1]

This integrity of outlook, so rare and valuable, explains and

---

[1] For this passage I have borrowed many expressions and opinions from an attractive and unfortunately unpublished study by Jean Laslever, O.P. on *L'Enfant*.

justifies the remark made by the composer of *Ma Mère l'Oye* to M.-D. Calvocoressi : " Does it never dawn on those people that I may be artificial by nature ? " " The child," said G. K. Chesterton, " regards everything, however complicated, with a simple delight. The falsely natural always insist on the distinction between the natural and the artificial. The truly natural take no account of such a distinction."

In Ravel's view, the " minuscule montre " of *Le Grillon* and the Catalan clock of *L'Heure Espagnole* are neither of them in the slightest artificial : but they are both mysterious—they are supernatural.

Ravel had the child's capacity for make-believe, by gazing at everything as though for the first time. Léon-Paul Fargue remembers what pleasure Ravel found in an exhibition of lacquers " at old Durand-Ruel's place in the Rue Laffitte. He showed the delight of a child taken to the ' Children's Paradise.' " [1]

He loved toys, minute knick-knacks, dwarf trees, and all manner of oddities, and convinced of their incomparable beauty, he either made everybody admire them at great length or he gave them as presents alike to grown-ups as to the children of his friends. Edouard Ravel had to spend several days in a nursing-home after an operation. With an air of infinite secrecy, his brother Maurice placed on his bedside table a little mechanical game of pelota, exquisitely put together.

His return from a journey to Venice was marked by presents to all his lady friends of baroque buckles in exquisite filigree work. I can still hear one of them exclaim as she opened her parcel : " Heavens, how ugly, but how kind of Ravel ! " But Ravel possessed the daring which belongs to the forerunners of fashion, and it was not long before this elegant lady was prominently wearing his gift.

His friends, knowing his passion, rivalled each other in ingenuity to help Ravel satisfy it. The " Belvédère " at Montfort-l'Amaury was thus enriched, during fifteen years, with some marvels—and some horrors : a mechanical nightin-gale, boats, bottle-imps, and flowers in spun glass. Hélène Jourdan-Morhange has described " the little sailing-boat which a secret winch caused to ride across waves of painted paper,

[1] Loc. cit.

and the miniature sofa, in flowered porcelain, which Germaine Tailleferre discovered . . ."[1]

One lovely evening in 1927, Léon Leyritz arrived at the house of Mme Marcelle Gerar, one of the composer's favourite interpreters,[2] to hear a rehearsal of the *Chansons Madécasses*. On the way he had bought from a pedlar a delightful little mechanical bird as a present for Ravel. The latter arrived late, as he usually did, and became absorbed in the toy without noticing the accompanist's desperate expression in his ecstasy at feeling the little metallic heart-beat. As a result, the rehearsal took place two hours late . . .

Ravel possessed in the highest degree the tyrannical and teasing character of the spoilt child. His friendship, like his music, made lavish use of anticipation and surprise. But it was exacting and admitted no excuses.

Incapable of envy and indifferent to the idea of being its object, he never answered, even by contempt, the kind of hatred which in any human group attaches itself to those different from the rest. He was only jealous in friendship ; but there he confessed himself to be terribly so. He found it hard to admit that he could be abandoned for anyone else. And as time did not count at all where he was concerned, he could not understand that it could count for his friends. For he did not allow a dependence on the clock, and with cunning virtuosity developed a genius for wasting his own time and making others waste theirs. On the other hand, no-one returned affection more generously—not in words, certainly, which he could not express ; but by delicate attentions and secretly rendered services. For just as he wanted everything about him to take place " as if it were a miracle," as Léon Leyritz has said, he himself took pains only to give pleasure by surprise.

Ravel was never heard to slander anybody. As for what he considered to be good in you, and the feelings you aroused in him, he waited for you to turn your back before he would give them expression. This reserve and frigidity which

---

[1] *Le Tombeau de Maurice Ravel.* Editions du Tambourinaire. M. Edouard Ravel decided to preserve the " Belvédère " as it was when his brother died.

[2] The *Madécasses* had first been sung by Mlle Madeleine Grey, a singer of whom Ravel had a particularly high opinion after her " creation " of the *Mélodies hébraïques* at the Concerts Pasdeloup.

normally characterized him only really left him in the company of children, young women or kittens, whose company he equally enjoyed. The incongruity of this association must be forgiven, in so far as it brings us to the " jardin féerique " of *Ma Mère l'Oye*, to the " green paradise of childhood loves," where desires are not accompanied by remorse ; where creatures are only loved for the beauty which they reflect ; and where Péguy's Holy Innocents play catch with their haloes.

" Naturally artificial " : in one sense child, in another dandy. Both existed simultaneously in Ravel. He could almost be described in the same words Baudelaire used for the bearing of a man of absolute genius who " had in him much of the dandy " and who " indulged with pleasure in the most material vanities of dandyism . . . He had the same apparent coldness," said Baudelaire, " the same icy cloak, hiding a reticent sensibility . . . Beneath the same show of egoism he had the same devotion to his secret friends and to the ideas of his choice . . . One of his supreme preoccupations was, I think, to conceal the turbulence of his heart and not to appear as a man of genius . ."

A common and secret attachment to dandyism alone can explain why the same description can with equal justice fit two artists and two men so different in other respects as were Eugène Delacroix and Maurice Ravel.

A discreet refinement in dress, an elegant frigidity, the refusal to allow a government the right to confer a decoration : all these traits fit the dandy. Add to them a certain liking for the fashionable world, which did not prevent a man of Ravel's calibre from letting the snobs see his distrust of facile vanities and the mechanics of success.

The idea of sacrificing or planning anything whatever in the interests of his career, even the idea that he could follow some career alongside his composition, never dawned on him. He was never rich and never dreamt of becoming so. He took absolutely no thought for his business affairs, and his careless-ness in money matters was equalled by his disinterestedness. His pupils can bear witness that he would accept no thanks for his lessons other than a gratitude which did not even have the right to express itself in words.

Above all, and this is supremely the mark of the dandy, Ravel seemed to be completely detached from his own work. His music only interested him as something to do—to do well. Once the work was finished, and the game over, he planned another exercise. It was all very well to listen to others' music with the hope, always too far off, of the " life-saving cigarette " ; but his own was always too much for him—he used to flee.

The mention of " game " brings us back to childhood—his true native land, the place of aimless yet ordered activity. The rule of the game, implying submission to the object, and the obstacle to be overcome—or to be created—were, and were to remain, the essential preoccupations of Ravel as craftsman. And when the final result, which motivates the form, does not spring from the arbitrary imposition of restraints, Ravel has to make use of creative imitation.

" Before I write a work," Satie used to say, " I wander round and round it with only myself for company." Ravel's perambulations were endless. His work took shape very slowly but was usually given final form fairly quickly.

A walk was the invariable preliminary for setting to work. Long expeditions in the woods, whatever the weather : nightly walks across Paris, which sometimes extended to the Bois de Boulogne and beyond. After a concert or dinner in town, he often persuaded several friends to visit one of the cafés in the Place du Havre, and then go on to the *Boeuf sur le toit* or the *Grand Ecart*. When he set out once more, on foot, for a destination unknown even to himself, it would often happen that an exhausted companion would be curtly dismissed, so that Ravel might pursue alone, with his lengthy stride, his indefatigable noctambulism.

But these wanderings had sudden ends. He would shut himself up and generally without hesitation produce a definitive manuscript, which was instantly seized by the printers. He composed in the greatest secret. Here again everything had to be done—or seem to be done—by a miracle. His piano and his study table bore no trace of his work and gave no evidence of preliminary drafts. Nothing in the hands or the pockets : the conjurer juggled away even the apparatus of his tricks. Things were accomplished as though the piano-keys manipulated the printers' dies at a distance.

Although no one ever saw him composing, he let us watch him orchestrating as much as we liked. When thus engaged, he always had to hand Widor's *Technique de l'Orchestre moderne* —an aid to memory which gave a list of trills and passages which could be played on every instrument. He also freely consulted the miniature scores of Saint-Saëns' Concertos for piano and orchestra and the symphonic poems of Richard Strauss.

When he was orchestrating, he continually went from the table to the piano, so that he could hear the parts of an instrumental group to better advantage by separating them out at the piano. According to him, he composed as much at the piano as at the table, claiming that for him the chief use of the piano was for orchestration.

Although for him the professional discipline was the Thesean thread 'to guide the mind in the maze of Art,' Ravel talked about it but little, and did not willingly enter into details of composition. Those young composers who used often to bring him their attempts and ask his advice, returned charmed by the simplicity of their reception and a little surprised by the severity of his uncompromising orthodoxy. " The truth of it is, you don't know anything. You must work." " Certainly, you are gifted ; but *everybody is gifted.* You needn't think I am any more so than anyone else. If each of you worked as I work, you could achieve the same results." " Choose a model ; imitate him. If you have nothing to say, all you can do is to copy. If you have got something to say, your personality will appear at its best in your unconscious infidelity."

Some of these phrases appear again, with the persistence of a " leitmotif," in conversations he had with his disciples, who in chronological order were Maurice Delage, the author of the present book, and Manuel Rosenthal. I believe that they appeared equally often in his discussions with the composers whom he voluntarily helped out of his experience and his kindly sympathy, particularly Vaughan Williams, Maurice Fouret, Nicolas Obouhow, Louis Durey, Germaine Taille-ferre, Lennox Berkeley and many others.

He loved Mozart with all his soul. He was devoted to Weber—" the great romantic "—to Liszt, Chopin, Bellini and

the Russians, with an obvious preference, though not a con-
spicuous one, for Borodin. Of the moderns, his admiration
went first and foremost to Chabrier, whom he linked with
Manet with the same feeling of affection. He did not understand
how the composer of the *Roi Malgré Lui* could be taxed with
vulgarity: " How can this composer be vulgar when even two
bars of his give away the author ? " He considered Charles
Gounod a forerunner of genius ; and, in spite of the slovenliness
of some of his writing, he did not hesitate to parallel *Mireille*
and *L'Arlésienne*, insisting how much the latter owed to the
former. Although by temperament and taste he was opposed
to the æsthetic of Bayreuth, he had never wanted to share in
those anti-Wagnerian frenzies which were the fashion in his
day. In his youth he had been charmed by the fairy aspects
of the *Ring* ; in later years he came to regard Wagner
" primarily for what he was throughout—a magnificent
musician." [1] As for Berlioz, whose genius was at the opposite
pole to his own, he praised his daring, which he considered
lacked merely the elements of a technique possessed by more
mediocre talents.

His liking for Saint-Saëns' music showed itself especially
towards the end of his second period—about 1910. His
Phaéton, *Le Rouet d'Omphale*, and his piano concertos and
chamber music showed him to be a great creator of values
in the strict sense as applied to musical structure.

As for Ravel's immediate contemporaries, mention has already
been made of the composer's feelings about Claude Debussy,
Stravinsky, Erik Satie and others.

Finally, his juniors, whom he treated with little respect when
he met them face to face, never had a surer defender, the
moment that he noticed that criticism of their daring was
really aimed at their youth. An article appearing in the
Nouvelles Littéraires in June 1927, shows in this respect a fine
generosity. In it, Marcel Delannoy is acclaimed as possessing
an " astonishing personality." Honegger " serves his art with
force, prudence and loyalty." Darius Milhaud's *Les malheurs
d'Orphée* is described as " an appealing, magnificent work,
the best its composer has written and one of the most accom-

---

[1] Reply to an enquiry on *Wagner et les Musiciens d'aujourd'hui*. *La Grande Revue*
10th May, 1909.

plished which our young School has produced for a very long time."

No pen can be expected to transmit the delightful spontaneity which lay at the heart of this little man of iron, who never truly revealed himself except to his intimate friends, and then not by effusions of which I have shown him to be incapable, but by sudden, unexpected confessions which manifested a candour and consciousness of self free alike from vanity and false modesty.

He said one day to Maurice and Nelly Delage : " It's lucky I've managed to write music, because I know perfectly well I should never have been able to do anything else . . ."

And to us, after the first performance of a contemporary work : " He can take liberties I would not allow myself, because he's less of a musician than I am."

To make a brief summary, the man was frank rather than eloquent ; polite rather than cordial ; with more sociability and vivacity than unselfconsciousness ; with more devotion to friendship than indulgence in friendliness ; and more sheer cleverness than all the rest put together.

Maurice Ravel as artist and man has always intrigued the critics because he slides from their grasp, eludes the intellectual analyst as he does the writer of romantic biographies. For Ravel's music is not in any way surrounded by those prickly hedges which, by hindering access to the work, give inter-preters full scope to hack their way through it. As a pure craftsman Ravel was utterly different from those æsthetes who, to use Nietzsche's charming expression, always fear " that they will be understood without much difficulty " and who are eager of their own accord to give their art a significance which lies far beyond its actual range.

Ravel's music does not intend to bestow on us a sense of rapture. This is the more true, in that his means coincide solely with the resources of his technique. He neither accepted nor thought of any others.

For this implacable classicist only wrote to write still better. It has been said that, like Baudelaire, he was ashamed of his heart. Yet, nevertheless, in Baudelaire, as here in Ravel, the hearts whose impulses have been ignored, continually pervade the whole of their work with the warmth of life.

"Here is a poet," said Baudelaire, "who claims that his poem has been written in accordance with his poetic system. He was assuredly a great genius and with more inspiration than anyone, if by inspiration one means energy, intellectual enthusiasm, and the ability to keep one's faculties alert. But he also loved work more than anyone else ; he willingly affirmed, he, the absolutely original artist, that originality is a matter of apprenticeship. Chance and obscurity were his two great enemies. Did he, by a strange and amusing vanity, make himself much less inspired than he naturally was ? Did he deliberately diminish the gifts which were freely his, in order to give the wider scope to will-power alone ? "

It is beyond doubt that Ravel had always passed himself off as " much less inspired than he naturally was." In ascribing to his industry alone the gifts of God, was he not more or less consciously satisfying a naive pride, and a childish Pelagianism? It is impossible to say. All that can be said is that we owe to his somewhat illusory artistic theory the concrete reality of his success.

His music would not be so finished, so smooth or so compact, if it were not free of all complicity. Ravel did not speculate about sentiment ; he worked out the sensation he wanted ; but, at the last extreme of tension and calculation some enchantment is set free which he did not invoke, and which the strictest attention to method would have been incapable of producing.

Here then is a man completely absorbed in the rules of the game, who neglected nothing in his aim to play it faultlessly, and who reasoned about his art as though he were the master of those powers which, unknown to himself, governed him. Genius of a musical order worked in him with supreme infallibility, secretly awaited and faithfully served by the most beautiful technique imaginable.

There are those who consider that Ravel's attitude to his work warrants the belittling of the range of his message, as though an artist does not invariably say more than he actually expresses ; as if man did not always excel himself when completely absorbed in his task !

One must not expect from Ravel works in which feeling is continually exaggerated by the violence of its expression. One must not ask Ravel to stir the dark waters of desire or willingly to reveal the gulfs of despair. If the lake which envelops the wondrous *Ondine* is deep, we gauge the depth by its limpidity. In a word, Ravel's magic—inasmuch as it exists—is still white magic.

For Ravel, as for every musician of the true French line, the real function of a composer is not and cannot be that of " thinking in music," which does not really mean anything, but to arrange the sounds " in a manner pleasing to the ear." Once such arrangement is arrived at by the senses and in the senses, then only can the work resound through the spirit.

Such is Ravel's law. It does not claim to be a new one : classicism fosters it ; its reward is its success.

Maurice Ravel with his favourite cat in his garden at Montfort (Mme. Jourdan Morhange).

CHRONOLOGICAL LIST OF
MAURICE RAVEL'S WORKS

1893	SÉRÉNADE GROTESQUE, piano, two hands	Unpublished
1894	BALLADE DE LA REINE MORTE D'AIMER (Roland de Marès), voice and piano	
1895	MENUET ANTIQUE[1], piano, two hands	Enoch
1895	UN GRAND SOMMEIL NOIR[2] (Verlaine), voice and piano	Unpublished
1895-6	LES SITES AURICULAIRES, two pianos, four hands (a) *Habañera*[3], 1895 (b) *Entre Cloches*, 1896	Unpublished
1896	SAINTE (Mallarmé), voice and piano	Durand
1898	DEUX EPIGRAMMES (Marot), voice and piano	Demets-Eschig
1898	SCHÉHÉRAZADE, Ouverture de féerie pour orchestre	Unpublished
1899	PAVANE POUR UNE INFANTE DÉFUNTE,[4] piano, two hands	Demets
1899	SI MORNE (Verhaeren), voice and piano	Unpublished
1901	MYRRHA (F. Beissier), cantata for the Prix de Rome	Unpublished
1901	JEUX D'EAU, piano, two hands	Demets-Eschig
1902	ALCYONE (A. and F. Adenis), cantata for the Prix de Rome	Unpublished
1902-3	STRING QUARTET IN F MAJOR	Durand
1903	ALYSSA, cantata for the Prix de Rome	Unpublished
1903	MANTEAU DE FLEURS[5] (P. Gravollet), voice and piano	Hamelle
1903	SCHÉHÉRAZADE (Tristan Klingsor), voice and orchestra (a) *Asie* (b) *La Flûte Enchantée* (c) *L'Indifférent*	Durand
1905	LE NOEL DES JOUETS[6] (M. Ravel), voice and piano	Mathot
1905	SONATINE, piano, two hands	Durand
1905	MIROIRS,[7] piano, two hands (a) *Noctuelles* (b) *Oiseaux tristes* (c) *Une barque sur l'Océan* (d) *Alborada del Gracioso* (e) *La Vallée des Cloches*	Demets-Eschig
1905-6	INTRODUCTION ET ALLEGRO, for harp with accompaniment of string quartet, flute and clarinet	Durand
1906	LES GRANDS VENTS VENUS D'OUTRE-MER (H. de Régnier), voice and piano	Durand
1906	HISTOIRES NATURELLES[8] (Jules Renard), voice and piano (a) *Le Paon* (*The Peacock*) (b) *Le Grillon* (*The Cricket*) (c) *Le Cygne* (*The Swan*) (d) *Le Martin-Pêcheur* (*The Kingfisher*) (e) *La Pintade* (*The Guinea-Hen*)	Durand
1907	SUR L'HERBE (Verlaine), voice and piano	Durand
1907	VOCALISE in the form of a Habañera	Leduc

[1] Orchestrated.
[2] The manuscript belongs to M. Lucien Garban.
[3] The *Habañera* has been used again in the *Rapsodie espagnole*.
[4] Orchestrated.
[5] Orchestrated.
[6] Orchestrated.
[7] *Une Barque sur l'Océan* and *Alborada del Gracioso* have been orchestrated.
[8] Orchestrated by Manuel Rosenthal.

1907	CINQ MÉLODIES POPULAIRES GRECQUES[9] (M.-D. Calvo-coressi), voice and piano	Durand
	(a) Le réveil de la mariée (The Bride's Awakening)	
	(b) Là-bas vers l'église (Down there by the church)	
	(c) Quel galant ! (What a handsome man !)	
	(d) Chanson des cueilleuses de lentisques (Song of the girls gathering lentils)	
	(e) Tout gai !	
1907	RAPSODIE ESPAGNOLE, for orchestra	Durand
	(a) Prélude à la nuit	
	(b) Malagueña	
	(c) Habañera	
	(d) Feria	
1907	L'HEURE ESPAGNOLE (Franc-Nohain), Musical comedy in one Act	Durand
1908	MA MERE L'OYE (Mother Goose)[10] children's pieces for piano, four hands	Durand
	(a) Pavane de la Belle au bois dormant (Pavane of the Sleeping Beauty)	
	(b) Petit Poucet (Hop o' my Thumb)	
	(c) Laideronette, Impératrice des Pagodes (Laideronette, Empress of the Pagodas)	
	(d) Les entretiens de la Belle et de la Bête (Conversations between Beauty and the Beast)	
	(e) Le jardin féerique (The Fairy Garden)	
1908	GASPARD DE LA NUIT three 'poems' for piano, two hands (after Aloysius Bertrand)	
	(a) Ondine	
	(b) Le Gibet	
	(c) Scarbo	
1909	MINUET on the name of Haydn, piano, two hands	Durand
1910	CHANTS POPULAIRES (FOLK SONGS)[11] with piano accompaniment	Jurgenson, Durand
	(a) Spanish	
	(b) French	
	(c) Italian	
	(d) Jewish	
	(e) Scottish	
	(f) Flemish	
	(g) Russian	
1911	VALSES NOBLES ET SENTIMENTALES[12], piano, two hands	Durand
1909-12	DAPHNIS ET CHLOÉ, choreographic symphony in three movements (Michel Fokine)	Durand
1912	MA MERE L'OYE[13], ballet (Maurice Ravel)	Durand
1913	TROIS POEMES DE STÉPHANE MALLARMÉ, for voice, piano, quartet, two flutes and two clarinets	Durand
	(a) Soupir	
	(b) Placet futile	
	(c) Surgi de la Croupe et du bond	
1913	PRÉLUDE[14], piano, two hands	Durand

Orchestrated ; (a) and (e) by the composer ; (b), (c) and (d) by Manuel Rosenthal.

[10] Orchestrated.

[11] These seven songs were performed during the competition of the *Maison du Lied*. The first four were first published with pieces appearing in a collection published by Jurgenson. The fourth is orchestrated. The last three are unpublished.

[12] Orchestrated. The orchestration forms the music for the ballet *Adélaïde, ou le langage des fleurs*.

[13] Transcription and adaptation of *Ma Mère l'Oye*, 1908.

[14] Composed for the sight reading test for the Piano Competition of the Paris Conservatoire (1913).

140

1913	A LA MANIÈRE DE . . . piano, two hands	Mathot
	(a) Borodine	
	(b) Chabrier	
1914	DEUX MÉLODIES HÉBRAIQUES[15], with piano accompaniment	Durand
	(a) Kaddisch	
	(b) L'Enigme éternelle	
1914	TRIO IN A MAJOR, for piano, violin and violoncello	Durand
1915	TROIS CHANSONS (M. Ravel), unaccompanied mixed chorus	Durand
	(a) Nicolette	
	(b) Trois beaux oiseaux du Paradis (Three fair birds of Paradise)	
	(c) Ronde	
1917	LE TOMBEAU DE COUPERIN[16], piano suite, two hands	Durand
	(a) Prélude	
	(b) Fugue	
	(c) Forlane	
	(d) Rigaudon	
	(e) Menuet	
	(f) Toccata	
1919	FRONTISPICE[17], piano, four hands	Feuillets d'art
1919-20	LA VALSE, choreographic poem for orchestra	Durand
1920-2	SONATA in four movements for violin and violoncello	Durand
1922	BERCEUSE,[18] on the name of Gabriel Fauré, for violin and piano	Durand
1924	RONSARD A SON AME,[19] (Ronsard), voice and piano	Durand
1924	TZIGANE,[20] rhapsody for violin and piano	Durand
1920-5	L'ENFANT ET LES SORTILEGES (Colette), lyrical fantasy in two parts	Durand
1925-6	CHANSONS MADÉCASSES (Parny), for voice, flute, violoncello and piano	Durand
	(a) Nahandove . . .	
	(b) Aoua !	
	(c) Il est doux . . .	
1927	REVES (L.-P. Fargue), voice and piano	Durand
1923-7	SONATA, in three movements, for violin and piano	Durand
1927	L'EVENTAIL DE JEANNE,[21] fanfare	Heugel
1928	BOLÉRO, for orchestra	Durand
1931	CONCERTO FOR LEFT HAND ALONE, piano and orchestra, in three movements	Durand
1931	CONCERTO IN G MAJOR, in three movements, for piano	Durand
1932	DON QUICHOTTE A DULCINÉE[22] (P. Morand), voice and piano	Durand
	(a) Chanson romantique	
	(b) Chanson épique	
	(c) Chanson à boire	

[15] Orchestrated.
[16] Orchestrated, with the exception of *Fugue* and *Toccata*.
[17] Written for Canudo's *Poème du Vardar*. S.P.503.
[18] Written for the supplement of one of the numbers of the *Revue Musicale* devoted to Gabriel Fauré.
[19] Supplement of one of the numbers of the *Revue Musicale—Le Tombeau de Ronsard*. Orchestrated.
[20] The accompaniment has been orchestrated.
[21] Precedes the ballet of this name—the concerted effort of ten composers.
[22] Orchestrated.

TRANSCRIPTIONS AND ORCHESTRATIONS

	Claude Debussy	PRÉLUDE A L'APRES-MIDI D'UN FAUNE transcription for two pianos	Jobert
1913	*Erik Satie*	PRÉLUDE DU FILS DES ÉTOILES, orchestration	Unpublished
1913	*Moussorgsky*	LA KHOVANTCHINA[23]	Unpublished
	Claude Debussy	SARABANDE, DANSE, orchestration	Jobert
1914	*Chopin*	NOCTURNE, ÉTUDE, VALSE,· orchestration	Unpublished
	Schumann	CARNAVAL[24], orchestration	Unpublished
1918	*Chabrier*	MENUET POMPEUX, orchestration	Enoch
1922	*Moussorgsky*	TABLEAUX D'UNE EXPOSITION, orchestration	Editions Russes de Musique

UNPUBLISHED WORKS AND MANUSCRIPTS

Although the composer's papers had not yet been classified at the time this book was written, it appeared reasonably certain that, apart from the works listed here, Maurice Ravel did not leave any works awaiting publication. *La Cloche Engloutie* and *Zaspiak bat* were only sketches, and *Morgiane* does not appear to have been even partially written.

The composer's most important manuscripts are distributed between M. Edouard Ravel, the firm of Durand, and M. Lucien Garban. It is due to their kindness that I have been able to reproduce certain excerpts in this book.

N.B.—Ravel disclaims his orchestration of *Une Barque sur l'Océan*. The firm of Eschig, in deference to the wish of the composer and his executors, have preserved the unpublished manuscript.

BIBLIOGRAPHY

I. BOOKS

M.-D. Calvocoressi	MUSIC AND BALLET IN PARIS AND LONDON	Faber & Faber
	CINQUANTE ANS DE MUSIQUE FRANCAISE 2 volumes	Librairie de France
A. Coeuroy	LA MUSIQUE FRANCAISE MODERNE	Delagrave
Ch. Malherbe	PROGRAMME DE QUATRE CONCERTS DE MUSIQUE FRANCAISE	Durand
J. Marnold	MUSICIENS D'AUTREFOIS ET D'AUJOURD'HUI	Dorbon
C. Mauclair	LA RELIGION DE LA MUSIQUE	Fischbacher
Roland-Manuel	MAURICE RAVEL ET SON ŒUVRE	Durand
	MAURICE RAVEL ET SON ŒUVRE DRAMATIQUE	Librairie de France
Pierre du Colombier and *Roland-Manuel*	LES ARTS (1900-1933)	Denöel et Steele

[23] A reorchestration of several passages of Rimsky-Korsakov's version.
[24] Two orchestrations made for the Russian Ballet.

Emile Vuillermoz	MUSIQUES D'AUJOURD'HUI	Delagrave
N.	MAURICE RAVEL	Grasset
V. Jankelevitch	MAURICE RAVEL	Rieder
George Dyson	THE NEW MUSIC	London, 1924
Cecil Gray	SURVEY OF CONTEMPORARY MUSIC	London, 1925
F. H. Shera	DEBUSSY AND RAVEL	O.U.P., 1938 3rd Imp.
Panndin	MODERN COMPOSERS (tr. Bonavia)	Dent, 1932
G. Jean Aubry	FRENCH MUSIC OF TO-DAY	

II. PERIODICALS

LA REVUE MUSICALE

	Special Number devoted to Maurice Ravel	1st April 1925
A. Suarès	POUR RAVEL	
T. Klingsor	RAVEL ET L'ART DE SON TEMPS	
Roland-Manuel	MAURICE RAVEL OU L'ESTHÉTIQUE DE L'IMPOSTURE	
E. Vuillermoz	LE STYLE ORCHESTRAL	
A. Casella	L'HARMONIE	
H. Gil-Marchex	LA TECHNIQUE DE PIANO	
A. Hoerée	LES MÉLODIES ET L'ŒUVRE LYRIQUE	
R. Chalupt	MAURICE RAVEL ET LES PRÉTEXTES LITTÉRAIRES DE SA MUSIQUE	
A. Coeuroy	IMAGES DE RAVEL AU MIROIR DES LETTRES	
G.-J. Aubry	HISTOIRES NATURELLES	Le Censeur, July 1907
G. Auric	L'ENFANT ET LES SORTILEGES	Nouvelles Littéraires, April 1925
	MAURICE RAVEL	Paris-Soir, 29th December 1937
J. Baruzi	RÉCITAL J. DUHEM	Le Ménestrel, 2nd March 1923
P. de Bréville	SCHÉHÉRAZADE	Mercure de France, July 1899
M. Brillant	L'ENFANT ET LES SORTILEGES	Le Correspondant, February 1926
R. Brussel	DAPHNIS ET CHLOÉ	Le Figaro, 9th June 1912
	LA MORT DE MAURICE RAVEL	Le Figaro, 29th December, 1937
E. Burlingame Hill	MAURICE RAVEL	Mercure Musical, 15th November 1906
M.-D. Calvocoressi	LE QUATUOR DE MAURICE RAVEL	La Revue Musicale, April 1904
	MAURICE RAVEL	Musical Times, December 1913
	LES HISTOIRES NATURELLES DE MAURICE RAVEL ET L'IMITATION DEBUSSYSTE	Grande Revue, May 1907
G. Carraud	HISTOIRES NATURELLES	La Liberté, 5th February 1907
	L'HEURE ESPAGNOLE	Liberté, 21st May 1911
	DAPHNIS	La Liberté, 11th June 1912

A. Casella	MAURICE RAVEL	Musica d'Oggi, Milan, March 1938
R. Chalupt	MA MERE L'OYE	La Phalange, May 1911
	L'HEURE ESPAGNOLE	ib. June 1911
	ADELAIDE	ib. June 1912
	DAPHNIS	ib. July 1912
J. Chantavoine	L'HEURE ESPAGNOLE	Revue Hebdomadaire, 24th June 1911
	DAPHNIS	Excelsior, 9th June 1912
A. Coeuroy	L'ENFANT ET LES SORTILEGES	Paris-Midi, 2nd February 1926
Covielle	MAURICE RAVEL ET LE PRIX DE ROME	Le Matin, 22nd May 1905
R. Dezarnaux	L'ENFANT ET LES SORTILEGES	La Liberté, 3rd February 1926
P. Donostia	HOMMAGE A MAURICE RAVEL	Gure Herria, Ustaritz, October-December, 1937
R. Dumesnil	MAURICE RAVEL	Mercure de France, 1st February 1938
L. P. Fargue	MAURICE RAVEL	Plaisir de France, August 1936
H. Gauthier-Villars (Willy)	P. LALO CONTRE RAVEL, L. LALOY PRO RAVEL	Mercure de France, 1st April 1907
	DAPHNIS	Comœdia illustré, 15th June 1912
H. Ghéon	L'HEURE ESPAGNOLE	N.R.F., 1st July 1911
A. George	L'ENFANT ET LES SORTILEGES	Nouvelles littéraires, February 1926
A. Honegger	L'ENFANT ET LES SORTILEGES	Musique et Théâtre, 15th April 1925
P. Lalo	MAURICE RAVEL	Le Temps, 13th June 1899
	LE QUATUOR	ib. 19th April 1904
	LE CONCOURS DE ROME	ib. 11th July 1905
	LES MIROIRS	ib. 30th January 1906
	MAURICE RAVEL ET LE DEBUSSYSME	ib. 19th March 1907
	UNE LETTRE DE MAURICE RAVEL	9th April 1907
	L'HEURE ESPAGNOLE	28th May 1911
	DAPHNIS	11th June 1912
	LE TOMBEAU DE COUPERIN	16th November 1922
	L'HEURE ESPAGNOLE, DAPHNIS	3rd February 1922
L. Laloy	MAURICE RAVEL	Mercure Musical, February and March 1907
	LA RAPSODIE ESPAGNOLE	Grande Revue, 25th March 1908
	GASPARD DE LA NUIT	ib. 25th January 1909
T. Lindenlaub	LA VALSE	Le Temps, 28th December 1920
H. Malherbe	L'ENFANT ET LES SORTILEGES	Le Temps, 3rd February 1926
A. Mantelli	MAURICE RAVEL	La Rassegna Musicale, Turin, No. 2, 1938

J. Marnold	LE QUATUOR DE MAURICE RAVEL	Mercure de France, April, 1904
	SCHÉHÉRAZADE	ib. July 1904
	LE SCANDALE DU PRIX DE ROME	ib. 1st June 1905
	L'AFFAIRE RAVEL	Revue musicale de Lyon, 1st May 1907 Mercure de France, 16th January 1908
	DAPHNIS ET CHLOÉ	Mercure de France, 16th August 1917
	L'ENFANT ET LES SORTILEGES	Mercure de France, 16th March 1926
C. Mauclair	A PROPOS DES BALLETS RUSSES	Courier musical, 15th June 1912
A. Messager	L'ENFANT ET LES SORTILEGES	Le Figaro, February 1926
D. Milhaud	MAURICE RAVEL	Ce Soir, 29th December 1937
R. O. Morris	MAURICE RAVEL	Music and Letters, July 1921
H. Prunières	L'ENFANT ET LES SORTILEGES	Revue Musicale, 1st April 1926
Roland-Manuel	MAURICE RAVEL	L'Echo Musical, February 1913
	LA VALSE	L'Eclair, December 1926
	L'ENFANT ET LES SORTILEGES	Le Ménestrel, 5th February 1906
	MAURICE RAVEL ET LA JEUNE ECOLE FRANCAISE	Nouvelles Literaires, June 1927
	LE GÉNIE DE MAURICE RAVEL	Temps présents, 7th January 1938
	RÉFLEXIONS SUR RAVEL	La Grande Revue, April 1938
Jacques Rivière	LA RAPSODIE ESPAGNOLE	N.R.F. February 1910
G. Samazeuilh	LES BALLETS RUSSES	Courrier Musical, 15th June 1912
	QUELQUES SOUVENIRS SUR MAURICE RAVEL	Le Temps, 29th December 1937
L. Vallas	LE NOUVEAU STYLE PIANISTIQUE	Revue musicale de Lyon, 6th January 1907
	ENCORE L'AFFAIRE RAVEL	ib. 14th April 1907
E. Vuillermoz	L'HEURE ESPAGNOLE	S.I.M. 15th June 1911
	MA MERE L'OYE	S.I.M. 15th February 1912
	DAPHNIS	S.I.M. 15th June 1912
	PORTRAIT DE MAURICE RAVEL	Cahiers d'aujourd'hui No. 10, 1922
	L'ENFANT ET LES SORTILEGES	Excelsior, 3rd February 1926
	MAURICE RAVEL EST MORT	Excelsior, 29th December 1937
	DÉFENDONS RAVEL!	Candide, 13th January 1938
	UNE GRANDE FIGURE DE LA MUSIQUE FRANCAISE	L'Illustration, 8th January 1938

MAURICE RAVEL'S WRITINGS

LA GRANDE REVUE	*Réponse à une enquête sur Wagner* (10th May, 1909).
REVUE MUSICALE DE LA S.I.M.	*Comptes rendus des Concerts Lamoureux et Colonne* (February 1912, March 1912, April 1912, November 1912).
LES CAHIERS D'AUJOURD'HUI	*A propos des Images de Claude Debussy* (No. 3, February, 1913).
COMŒDIA ILLUSTRÉ	*Reprise de Boris Godounoff* (1913).
LA REVUE MUSICALE	*Les Mélodies de Gabriel Fauré.*
LA REVUE MUSICALE	*Special number devoted to Gabriel Fauré* (1922), Etc., etc.

PAINTINGS, Etc.

G. d'Espagnat	UN GROUPE DE MUSICIENS (Oil-painting in the Opéra Museum).
L. Leyritz	BUST (Opéra).
H. Manguin	PORTRAIT (Oil-painting).
Luc-Albert Moreau	VARIOUS PORTRAITS (Engravings and drawings).
Louise Ochsé	BUST (Marble).
A. Ouvré	VARIOUS PORTRAITS.

Index

Index

Index

Index

A CATALOGUE OF SELECTED DOVER BOOKS
IN ALL FIELDS OF INTEREST

A CATALOGUE OF SELECTED DOVER BOOKS
IN ALL FIELDS OF INTEREST

AMERICA'S OLD MASTERS, James T. Flexner. Four men emerged unexpectedly from provincial 18th century America to leadership in European art: Benjamin West, J. S. Copley, C. R. Peale, Gilbert Stuart. Brilliant coverage of lives and contributions. Revised, 1967 edition. 69 plates. 365pp. of text.
21806-6 Paperbound $3.00

FIRST FLOWERS OF OUR WILDERNESS: AMERICAN PAINTING, THE COLONIAL PERIOD, James T. Flexner. Painters, and regional painting traditions from earliest Colonial times up to the emergence of Copley, West and Peale Sr., Foster, Gustavus Hesselius, Feke, John Smibert and many anonymous painters in the primitive manner. Engaging presentation, with 162 illustrations. xxii + 368pp.
22180-6 Paperbound $3.50

THE LIGHT OF DISTANT SKIES: AMERICAN PAINTING, 1760-1835, James T. Flexner. The great generation of early American painters goes to Europe to learn and to teach: West, Copley, Gilbert Stuart and others. Allston, Trumbull, Morse; also contemporary American painters—primitives, derivatives, academics—who remained in America. 102 illustrations. xiii + 306pp.
22179-2 Paperbound $3.00

A HISTORY OF THE RISE AND PROGRESS OF THE ARTS OF DESIGN IN THE UNITED STATES, William Dunlap. Much the richest mine of information on early American painters, sculptors, architects, engravers, miniaturists, etc. The only source of information for scores of artists, the major primary source for many others. Unabridged reprint of rare original 1834 edition, with new introduction by James T. Flexner, and 394 new illustrations. Edited by Rita Weiss. 6⅝ x 9⅝.
21695-0, 21696-9, 21697-7 Three volumes, Paperbound $13.50

EPOCHS OF CHINESE AND JAPANESE ART, Ernest F. Fenollosa. From primitive Chinese art to the 20th century, thorough history, explanation of every important art period and form, including Japanese woodcuts; main stress on China and Japan, but Tibet, Korea also included. Still unexcelled for its detailed, rich coverage of cultural background, aesthetic elements, diffusion studies, particularly of the historical period. 2nd, 1913 edition. 242 illustrations. lii + 439pp. of text.
20364-6, 20365-4 Two volumes, Paperbound $6.00

THE GENTLE ART OF MAKING ENEMIES, James A. M. Whistler. Greatest wit of his day deflates Oscar Wilde, Ruskin, Swinburne; strikes back at inane critics, exhibitions, art journalism; aesthetics of impressionist revolution in most striking form. Highly readable classic by great painter. Reproduction of edition designed by Whistler. Introduction by Alfred Werner. xxxvi + 334pp.
21875-9 Paperbound $2.50

VISUAL ILLUSIONS: THEIR CAUSES, CHARACTERISTICS, AND APPLICATIONS, Matthew Luckiesh. Thorough description and discussion of optical illusion, geometric and perspective, particularly; size and shape distortions, illusions of color, of motion; natural illusions; use of illusion in art and magic, industry, etc. Most useful today with op art, also for classical art. Scores of effects illustrated. Introduction by William H. Ittleson. 100 illustrations. xxi + 252pp.

21530-X Paperbound $2.00

A HANDBOOK OF ANATOMY FOR ART STUDENTS, Arthur Thomson. Thorough, virtually exhaustive coverage of skeletal structure, musculature, etc. Full text, supplemented by anatomical diagrams and drawings and by photographs of undraped figures. Unique in its comparison of male and female forms, pointing out differences of contour, texture, form. 211 figures, 40 drawings, 86 photographs. xx + 459pp. 5⅜ x 8⅜.

21163-0 Paperbound $3.50

150 MASTERPIECES OF DRAWING, Selected by Anthony Toney. Full page reproductions of drawings from the early 16th to the end of the 18th century, all beautifully reproduced: Rembrandt, Michelangelo, Dürer, Fragonard, Urs, Graf, Wouwerman, many others. First-rate browsing book, model book for artists. xviii + 150pp. 8⅜ x 11¼.

21032-4 Paperbound $2.50

THE LATER WORK OF AUBREY BEARDSLEY, Aubrey Beardsley. Exotic, erotic, ironic masterpieces in full maturity: Comedy Ballet, Venus and Tannhauser, Pierrot, Lysistrata, Rape of the Lock, Savoy material, Ali Baba, Volpone, etc. This material revolutionized the art world, and is still powerful, fresh, brilliant. With *The Early Work*, all Beardsley's finest work. 174 plates, 2 in color. xiv + 176pp. 8⅛ x 11.

21817-1 Paperbound $3.00

DRAWINGS OF REMBRANDT, Rembrandt van Rijn. Complete reproduction of fabulously rare edition by Lippmann and Hofstede de Groot, completely reedited, updated, improved by Prof. Seymour Slive, Fogg Museum. Portraits, Biblical sketches, landscapes, Oriental types, nudes, episodes from classical mythology—All Rembrandt's fertile genius. Also selection of drawings by his pupils and followers. "Stunning volumes," *Saturday Review*. 550 illustrations. lxxviii + 552pp. 9⅛ x 12¼.

21485-0, 21486-9 Two volumes, Paperbound $7.00

THE DISASTERS OF WAR, Francisco Goya. One of the masterpieces of Western civilization—83 etchings that record Goya's shattering, bitter reaction to the Napoleonic war that swept through Spain after the insurrection of 1808 and to war in general. Reprint of the first edition, with three additional plates from Boston's Museum of Fine Arts. All plates facsimile size. Introduction by Philip Hofer, Fogg Museum. v + 97pp. 9⅜ x 8¼.

21872-4 Paperbound $2.00

GRAPHIC WORKS OF ODILON REDON. Largest collection of Redon's graphic works ever assembled: 172 lithographs, 28 etchings and engravings, 9 drawings. These include some of his most famous works. All the plates from *Odilon Redon: oeuvre graphique complet*, plus additional plates. New introduction and caption translations by Alfred Werner. 209 illustrations. xxvii + 209pp. 9⅛ x 12¼.

21966-8 Paperbound $4.00

DESIGN BY ACCIDENT; A BOOK OF "ACCIDENTAL EFFECTS" FOR ARTISTS AND DESIGNERS, James F. O'Brien. Create your own unique, striking, imaginative effects by "controlled accident" interaction of materials: paints and lacquers, oil and water based paints, splatter, crackling materials, shatter, similar items. Everything you do will be different; first book on this limitless art, so useful to both fine artist and commercial artist. Full instructions. 192 plates showing "accidents," 8 in color. viii + 215pp. 8⅜ x 11¼.   21942-9 Paperbound $3.50

THE BOOK OF SIGNS, Rudolf Koch. Famed German type designer draws 493 beautiful symbols: religious, mystical, alchemical, imperial, property marks, runes, etc. Remarkable fusion of traditional and modern. Good for suggestions of timelessness, smartness, modernity. Text. vi + 104pp. 6⅛ x 9¼.
                                        20162-7 Paperbound $1.25

HISTORY OF INDIAN AND INDONESIAN ART, Ananda K. Coomaraswamy. An unabridged republication of one of the finest books by a great scholar in Eastern art. Rich in descriptive material, history, social backgrounds; Sunga reliefs, Rajput paintings, Gupta temples, Burmese frescoes, textiles, jewelry, sculpture, etc. 400 photos. viii + 423pp. 6⅜ x 9¾.   21436-2 Paperbound $4.00

PRIMITIVE ART, Franz Boas. America's foremost anthropologist surveys textiles, ceramics, woodcarving, basketry, metalwork, etc.; patterns, technology, creation of symbols, style origins. All areas of world, but very full on Northwest Coast Indians. More than 350 illustrations of baskets, boxes, totem poles, weapons, etc. 378 pp.
                                        20025-6 Paperbound $3.00

THE GENTLEMAN AND CABINET MAKER'S DIRECTOR, Thomas Chippendale. Full reprint (third edition, 1762) of most influential furniture book of all time, by master cabinetmaker. 200 plates, illustrating chairs, sofas, mirrors, tables, cabinets, plus 24 photographs of surviving pieces. Biographical introduction by N. Bienenstock. vi + 249pp. 9⅞ x 12¾.   21601-2 Paperbound $4.00

AMERICAN ANTIQUE FURNITURE, Edgar G. Miller, Jr. The basic coverage of all American furniture before 1840. Individual chapters cover type of furniture— clocks, tables, sideboards, etc.—chronologically, with inexhaustible wealth of data. More than 2100 photographs, all identified, commented on. Essential to all early American collectors. Introduction by H. E. Keyes. vi + 1106pp. 7⅞ x 10¾.
            21599-7, 21600-4 Two volumes, Paperbound $11.00

PENNSYLVANIA DUTCH AMERICAN FOLK ART, Henry J. Kauffman. 279 photos, 28 drawings of tulipware, Fraktur script, painted tinware, toys, flowered furniture, quilts, samplers, hex signs, house interiors, etc. Full descriptive text. Excellent for tourist, rewarding for designer, collector. Map. 146pp. 7⅞ x 10¾.
                                        21205-X Paperbound $2.50

EARLY NEW ENGLAND GRAVESTONE RUBBINGS, Edmund V. Gillon, Jr. 43 photographs, 226 carefully reproduced rubbings show heavily symbolic, sometimes macabre early gravestones, up to early 19th century. Remarkable early American primitive art, occasionally strikingly beautiful; always powerful. Text. xxvi + 207pp. 8⅜ x 11¼.   21380-3 Paperbound $3.50

ALPHABETS AND ORNAMENTS, Ernst Lehner. Well-known pictorial source for decorative alphabets, script examples, cartouches, frames, decorative title pages, calligraphic initials, borders, similar material. 14th to 19th century, mostly European. Useful in almost any graphic arts designing, varied styles. 750 illustrations. 256pp. 7 x 10. 21905-4 Paperbound $4.00

PAINTING: A CREATIVE APPROACH, Norman Colquhoun. For the beginner simple guide provides an instructive approach to painting: major stumbling blocks for beginner; overcoming them, technical points; paints and pigments; oil painting; watercolor and other media and color. New section on "plastic" paints. Glossary. Formerly *Paint Your Own Pictures.* 221pp. 22000-1 Paperbound $1.75

THE ENJOYMENT AND USE OF COLOR, Walter Sargent. Explanation of the relations between colors themselves and between colors in nature and art, including hundreds of little-known facts about color values, intensities, effects of high and low illumination, complementary colors. Many practical hints for painters, references to great masters. 7 color plates, 29 illustrations. x + 274pp.
20944-X Paperbound $2.75

THE NOTEBOOKS OF LEONARDO DA VINCI, compiled and edited by Jean Paul Richter. 1566 extracts from original manuscripts reveal the full range of Leonardo's versatile genius: all his writings on painting, sculpture, architecture, anatomy, astronomy, geography, topography, physiology, mining, music, etc., in both Italian and English, with 186 plates of manuscript pages and more than 500 additional drawings. Includes studies for the Last Supper, the lost Sforza monument, and other works. Total of xlvii + 866pp. 7⅞ x 10¾.
22572-0, 22573-9 Two volumes, Paperbound $10.00

MONTGOMERY WARD CATALOGUE OF 1895. Tea gowns, yards of flannel and pillow-case lace, stereoscopes, books of gospel hymns, the New Improved Singer Sewing Machine, side saddles, milk skimmers, straight-edged razors, high-button shoes, spittoons, and on and on . . . listing some 25,000 items, practically all illustrated. Essential to the shoppers of the 1890's, it is our truest record of the spirit of the period. Unaltered reprint of Issue No. 57, Spring and Summer 1895. Introduction by Boris Emmet. Innumerable illustrations. xiii + 624pp. 8½ x 11⅝.
22377-9 Paperbound $6.95

THE CRYSTAL PALACE EXHIBITION ILLUSTRATED CATALOGUE (LONDON, 1851). One of the wonders of the modern world—the Crystal Palace Exhibition in which all the nations of the civilized world exhibited their achievements in the arts and sciences—presented in an equally important illustrated catalogue. More than 1700 items pictured with accompanying text—ceramics, textiles, cast-iron work, carpets, pianos, sleds, razors, wall-papers, billiard tables, beehives, silverware and hundreds of other artifacts—represent the focal point of Victorian culture in the Western World. Probably the largest collection of Victorian decorative art ever assembled— indispensable for antiquarians and designers. Unabridged republication of the Art-Journal Catalogue of the Great Exhibition of 1851, with all terminal essays. New introduction by John Gloag, F.S.A. xxxiv + 426pp. 9 x 12.
22503-8 Paperbound $4.50

A HISTORY OF COSTUME, Carl Köhler. Definitive history, based on surviving pieces of clothing primarily, and paintings, statues, etc. secondarily. Highly readable text, supplemented by 594 illustrations of costumes of the ancient Mediterranean peoples, Greece and Rome, the Teutonic prehistoric period; costumes of the Middle Ages, Renaissance, Baroque, 18th and 19th centuries. Clear, measured patterns are provided for many clothing articles. Approach is practical throughout. Enlarged by Emma von Sichart. 464pp. 21030-8 Paperbound $3.50

ORIENTAL RUGS, ANTIQUE AND MODERN, Walter A. Hawley. A complete and authoritative treatise on the Oriental rug—where they are made, by whom and how, designs and symbols, characteristics in detail of the six major groups, how to distinguish them and how to buy them. Detailed technical data is provided on periods, weaves, warps, wefts, textures, sides, ends and knots, although no technical background is required for an understanding. 11 color plates, 80 halftones, 4 maps. vi + 320pp. $6\frac{1}{8}$ x $9\frac{1}{8}$. 22366-3 Paperbound $5.00

TEN BOOKS ON ARCHITECTURE, Vitruvius. By any standards the most important book on architecture ever written. Early Roman discussion of aesthetics of building, construction methods, orders, sites, and every other aspect of architecture has inspired, instructed architecture for about 2,000 years. Stands behind Palladio, Michelangelo, Bramante, Wren, countless others. Definitive Morris H. Morgan translation. 68 illustrations. xii + 331pp. 20645-9 Paperbound $2.50

THE FOUR BOOKS OF ARCHITECTURE, Andrea Palladio. Translated into every major Western European language in the two centuries following its publication in 1570, this has been one of the most influential books in the history of architecture. Complete reprint of the 1738 Isaac Ware edition. New introduction by Adolf Placzek, Columbia Univ. 216 plates. xxii + 110pp. of text. $9\frac{1}{2}$ x $12\frac{3}{4}$. 21308-0 Clothbound $10.00

STICKS AND STONES: A STUDY OF AMERICAN ARCHITECTURE AND CIVILIZATION, Lewis Mumford.One of the great classics of American cultural history. American architecture from the medieval-inspired earliest forms to the early 20th century; evolution of structure and style, and reciprocal influences on environment. 21 photographic illustrations. 238pp. 20202-X Paperbound $2.00

THE AMERICAN BUILDER'S COMPANION, Asher Benjamin. The most widely used early 19th century architectural style and source book, for colonial up into Greek Revival periods. Extensive development of geometry of carpentering, construction of sashes, frames, doors, stairs; plans and elevations of domestic and other buildings. Hundreds of thousands of houses were built according to this book, now invaluable to historians, architects, restorers, etc. 1827 edition. 59 plates. 114pp. $7\frac{7}{8}$ x $10\frac{3}{4}$. 22236-5 Paperbound $3.00

DUTCH HOUSES IN THE HUDSON VALLEY BEFORE 1776, Helen Wilkinson Reynolds. The standard survey of the Dutch colonial house and outbuildings, with constructional features, decoration, and local history associated with individual homesteads. Introduction by Franklin D. Roosevelt. Map. 150 illustrations. 469pp. $6\frac{5}{8}$ x $9\frac{1}{4}$. 21469-9 Paperbound $4.00

THE ARCHITECTURE OF COUNTRY HOUSES, Andrew J. Downing. Together with Vaux's *Villas and Cottages* this is the basic book for Hudson River Gothic architecture of the middle Victorian period. Full, sound discussions of general aspects of housing, architecture, style, decoration, furnishing, together with scores of detailed house plans, illustrations of specific buildings, accompanied by full text. Perhaps the most influential single American architectural book. 1850 edition. Introduction by J. Stewart Johnson. 321 figures, 34 architectural designs. xvi + 560pp.

22003-6 Paperbound $4.00

LOST EXAMPLES OF COLONIAL ARCHITECTURE, John Mead Howells. Full-page photographs of buildings that have disappeared or been so altered as to be denatured, including many designed by major early American architects. 245 plates. xvii + 248pp. 7⅞ x 10¾. 21143-6 Paperbound $3.50

DOMESTIC ARCHITECTURE OF THE AMERICAN COLONIES AND OF THE EARLY REPUBLIC, Fiske Kimball. Foremost architect and restorer of Williamsburg and Monticello covers nearly 200 homes between 1620-1825. Architectural details, construction, style features, special fixtures, floor plans, etc. Generally considered finest work in its area. 219 illustrations of houses, doorways, windows, capital mantels. xx + 314pp. 7⅞ x 10¾. 21743-4 Paperbound $4.00

EARLY AMERICAN ROOMS: 1650-1858, edited by Russell Hawes Kettell. Tour of 12 rooms, each representative of a different era in American history and each furnished, decorated, designed and occupied in the style of the era. 72 plans and elevations, 8-page color section, etc., show fabrics, wall papers, arrangements, etc. Full descriptive text. xvii + 200pp. of text. 8⅜ x 11¼.

21633-0 Paperbound $5.00

THE FITZWILLIAM VIRGINAL BOOK, edited by J. Fuller Maitland and W. B. Squire. Full modern printing of famous early 17th-century ms. volume of 300 works by Morley, Byrd, Bull, Gibbons, etc. For piano or other modern keyboard instrument; easy to read format. xxxvi + 938pp. 8⅜ x 11.

21068-5, 21069-3 Two volumes, Paperbound $10.00

KEYBOARD MUSIC, Johann Sebastian Bach. Bach Gesellschaft edition. A rich selection of Bach's masterpieces for the harpsichord: the six English Suites, six French Suites, the six Partitas (Clavierübung part I), the Goldberg Variations (Clavierübung part IV), the fifteen Two-Part Inventions and the fifteen Three-Part Sinfonias. Clearly reproduced on large sheets with ample margins; eminently playable. vi + 312pp. 8⅛ x 11. 22360-4 Paperbound $5.00

THE MUSIC OF BACH: AN INTRODUCTION, Charles Sanford Terry. A fine, nontechnical introduction to Bach's music, both instrumental and vocal. Covers organ music, chamber music, passion music, other types. Analyzes themes, developments, innovations. x + 114pp. 21075-8 Paperbound $1.25

BEETHOVEN AND HIS NINE SYMPHONIES, Sir George Grove. Noted British musicologist provides best history, analysis, commentary on symphonies. Very thorough, rigorously accurate; necessary to both advanced student and amateur music lover. 436 musical passages. vii + 407 pp. 20334-4 Paperbound $2.75

JOHANN SEBASTIAN BACH, Philipp Spitta. One of the great classics of musicology, this definitive analysis of Bach's music (and life) has never been surpassed. Lucid, nontechnical analyses of hundreds of pieces (30 pages devoted to St. Matthew Passion, 26 to B Minor Mass). Also includes major analysis of 18th-century music. 450 musical examples. 40-page musical supplement. Total of xx + 1799pp.
(EUK) 22278-0, 22279-9 Two volumes, Clothbound $17.50

MOZART AND HIS PIANO CONCERTOS, Cuthbert Girdlestone. The only full-length study of an important area of Mozart's creativity. Provides detailed analyses of all 23 concertos, traces inspirational sources. 417 musical examples. Second edition. 509pp. (USO) 21271-8 Paperbound $3.50

THE PERFECT WAGNERITE: A COMMENTARY ON THE NIBLUNG'S RING, George Bernard Shaw. Brilliant and still relevant criticism in remarkable essays on Wagner's Ring cycle, Shaw's ideas on political and social ideology behind the plots, role of Leitmotifs, vocal requisites, etc. Prefaces. xxi + 136pp.
21707-8 Paperbound $1.50

DON GIOVANNI, W. A. Mozart. Complete libretto, modern English translation; biographies of composer and librettist; accounts of early performances and critical reaction. Lavishly illustrated. All the material you need to understand and appreciate this great work. Dover Opera Guide and Libretto Series; translated and introduced by Ellen Bleiler. 92 illustrations. 209pp.
21134-7 Paperbound $1.50

HIGH FIDELITY SYSTEMS: A LAYMAN'S GUIDE, Roy F. Allison. All the basic information you need for setting up your own audio system: high fidelity and stereo record players, tape records, F.M. Connections, adjusting tone arm, cartridge, checking needle alignment, positioning speakers, phasing speakers, adjusting hums, trouble-shooting, maintenance, and similar topics. Enlarged 1965 edition. More than 50 charts, diagrams, photos. iv + 91pp. 21514-8 Paperbound $1.25

REPRODUCTION OF SOUND, Edgar Villchur. Thorough coverage for laymen of high fidelity systems, reproducing systems in general, needles, amplifiers, preamps, loudspeakers, feedback, explaining physical background. "A rare talent for making technicalities vividly comprehensible," R. Darrell, *High Fidelity*. 69 figures. iv + 92pp. 21515-6 Paperbound $1.25

HEAR ME TALKIN' TO YA: THE STORY OF JAZZ AS TOLD BY THE MEN WHO MADE IT, Nat Shapiro and Nat Hentoff. Louis Armstrong, Fats Waller, Jo Jones, Clarence Williams, Billy Holiday, Duke Ellington, Jelly Roll Morton and dozens of other jazz greats tell how it was in Chicago's South Side, New Orleans, depression Harlem and the modern West Coast as jazz was born and grew. xvi + 429pp.
21726-4 Paperbound $2.50

FABLES OF AESOP, translated by Sir Roger L'Estrange. A reproduction of the very rare 1931 Paris edition; a selection of the most interesting fables, together with 50 imaginative drawings by Alexander Calder. v + 128pp. 6½x9¼.
21780-9 Paperbound $1.50

AGAINST THE GRAIN (A REBOURS), Joris K. Huysmans. Filled with weird images, evidences of a bizarre imagination, exotic experiments with hallucinatory drugs, rich tastes and smells and the diversions of its sybarite hero Duc Jean des Esseintes, this classic novel pushed 19th-century literary decadence to its limits. Full unabridged edition. Do not confuse this with abridged editions generally sold. Introduction by Havelock Ellis. xlix + 206pp. 22190-3 Paperbound $2.00

VARIORUM SHAKESPEARE: HAMLET. Edited by Horace H. Furness; a landmark of American scholarship. Exhaustive footnotes and appendices treat all doubtful words and phrases, as well as suggested critical emendations throughout the play's history. First volume contains editor's own text, collated with all Quartos and Folios. Second volume contains full first Quarto, translations of Shakespeare's sources (Belleforest, and Saxo Grammaticus), Der Bestrafte Brudermord, and many essays on critical and historical points of interest by major authorities of past and present. Includes details of staging and costuming over the years. By far the best edition available for serious students of Shakespeare. Total of xx + 905pp.
21004-9, 21005-7, 2 volumes, Paperbound $7.00

A LIFE OF WILLIAM SHAKESPEARE, Sir Sidney Lee. This is the standard life of Shakespeare, summarizing everything known about Shakespeare and his plays. Incredibly rich in material, broad in coverage, clear and judicious, it has served thousands as the best introduction to Shakespeare. 1931 edition. 9 plates. xxix + 792pp. (USO) 21967-4 Paperbound $3.75

MASTERS OF THE DRAMA, John Gassner. Most comprehensive history of the drama in print, covering every tradition from Greeks to modern Europe and America, including India, Far East, etc. Covers more than 800 dramatists, 2000 plays, with biographical material, plot summaries, theatre history, criticism, etc. "Best of its kind in English," New Republic. 77 illustrations. xxii + 890pp.
20100-7 Clothbound $8.50

THE EVOLUTION OF THE ENGLISH LANGUAGE, George McKnight. The growth of English, from the 14th century to the present. Unusual, non-technical account presents basic information in very interesting form: sound shifts, change in grammar and syntax, vocabulary growth, similar topics. Abundantly illustrated with quotations. Formerly Modern English in the Making. xii + 590pp.
21932-1 Paperbound $3.50

AN ETYMOLOGICAL DICTIONARY OF MODERN ENGLISH, Ernest Weekley. Fullest, richest work of its sort, by foremost British lexicographer. Detailed word histories, including many colloquial and archaic words; extensive quotations. Do not confuse this with the Concise Etymological Dictionary, which is much abridged. Total of xxvii + 830pp. 6½ x 9¼.
21873-2, 21874-0 Two volumes, Paperbound $6.00

FLATLAND: A ROMANCE OF MANY DIMENSIONS, E. A. Abbott. Classic of science-fiction explores ramifications of life in a two-dimensional world, and what happens when a three-dimensional being intrudes. Amusing reading, but also useful as introduction to thought about hyperspace. Introduction by Banesh Hoffmann. 16 illustrations. xx + 103pp. 20001-9 Paperbound $1.00

POEMS OF ANNE BRADSTREET, edited with an introduction by Robert Hutchinson. A new selection of poems by America's first poet and perhaps the first significant woman poet in the English language. 48 poems display her development in works of considerable variety—love poems, domestic poems, religious meditations, formal elegies, "quaternions," etc. Notes, bibliography. viii + 222pp.

22160-1 Paperbound $2.00

THREE GOTHIC NOVELS: THE CASTLE OF OTRANTO BY HORACE WALPOLE; VATHEK BY WILLIAM BECKFORD; THE VAMPYRE BY JOHN POLIDORI, WITH FRAGMENT OF A NOVEL BY LORD BYRON, edited by E. F. Bleiler. The first Gothic novel, by Walpole; the finest Oriental tale in English, by Beckford; powerful Romantic supernatural story in versions by Polidori and Byron. All extremely important in history of literature; all still exciting, packed with supernatural thrills, ghosts, haunted castles, magic, etc. xl + 291pp.

21232-7 Paperbound $2.00

THE BEST TALES OF HOFFMANN, E. T. A. Hoffmann. 10 of Hoffmann's most important stories, in modern re-editings of standard translations: Nutcracker and the King of Mice, Signor Formica, Automata, The Sandman, Rath Krespel, The Golden Flowerpot, Master Martin the Cooper, The Mines of Falun, The King's Betrothed, A New Year's Eve Adventure. 7 illustrations by Hoffmann. Edited by E. F. Bleiler. xxxix + 419pp.

21793-0 Paperbound $2.50

GHOST AND HORROR STORIES OF AMBROSE BIERCE, Ambrose Bierce. 23 strikingly modern stories of the horrors latent in the human mind: The Eyes of the Panther, The Damned Thing, An Occurrence at Owl Creek Bridge, An Inhabitant of Carcosa, etc., plus the dream-essay, Visions of the Night. Edited by E. F. Bleiler. xxii + 199pp.

20767-6 Paperbound $1.50

BEST GHOST STORIES OF J. S. LeFANU, J. Sheridan LeFanu. Finest stories by Victorian master often considered greatest supernatural writer of all. Carmilla, Green Tea, The Haunted Baronet, The Familiar, and 12 others. Most never before available in the U. S. A. Edited by E. F. Bleiler. 8 illustrations from Victorian publications. xvii + 467pp.

20415-4 Paperbound $3.00

THE TIME STREAM, THE GREATEST ADVENTURE, AND THE PURPLE SAPPHIRE—THREE SCIENCE FICTION NOVELS, John Taine (Eric Temple Bell). Great American mathematician was also foremost science fiction novelist of the 1920's. *The Time Stream,* one of all-time classics, uses concepts of circular time; *The Greatest Adventure,* incredibly ancient biological experiments from Antarctica threaten to escape; The *Purple Sapphire,* superscience, lost races in Central Tibet, survivors of the Great Race. 4 illustrations by Frank R. Paul. v + 532pp.

21180-0 Paperbound $3.00

SEVEN SCIENCE FICTION NOVELS, H. G. Wells. The standard collection of the great novels. Complete, unabridged. *First Men in the Moon, Island of Dr. Moreau, War of the Worlds, Food of the Gods, Invisible Man, Time Machine, In the Days of the Comet.* Not only science fiction fans, but every educated person owes it to himself to read these novels. 1015pp.

20264-X Clothbound $5.00

LAST AND FIRST MEN AND STAR MAKER, TWO SCIENCE FICTION NOVELS, Olaf Stapledon. Greatest future histories in science fiction. In the first, human intelligence is the "hero," through strange paths of evolution, interplanetary invasions, incredible technologies, near extinctions and reemergences. Star Maker describes the quest of a band of star rovers for intelligence itself, through time and space: weird inhuman civilizations, crustacean minds, symbiotic worlds, etc. Complete, unabridged. v + 438pp.   21962-3 Paperbound $2.50

THREE PROPHETIC NOVELS, H. G. WELLS. Stages of a consistently planned future for mankind. *When the Sleeper Wakes*, and *A Story of the Days to Come*, anticipate *Brave New World* and *1984*, in the 21st Century; *The Time Machine*, only complete version in print, shows farther future and the end of mankind. All show Wells's greatest gifts as storyteller and novelist. Edited by E. F. Bleiler. x + 335pp.   (USO) 20605-X Paperbound $2.25

THE DEVIL'S DICTIONARY, Ambrose Bierce. America's own Oscar Wilde—Ambrose Bierce—offers his barbed iconoclastic wisdom in over 1,000 definitions hailed by H. L. Mencken as "some of the most gorgeous witticisms in the English language." 145pp.   20487-1 Paperbound $1.25

MAX AND MORITZ, Wilhelm Busch. Great children's classic, father of comic strip, of two bad boys, Max and Moritz. Also Ker and Plunk (Plisch und Plumm), Cat and Mouse, Deceitful Henry, Ice-Peter, The Boy and the Pipe, and five other pieces. Original German, with English translation. Edited by H. Arthur Klein; translations by various hands and H. Arthur Klein. vi + 216pp.
20181-3 Paperbound $2.00

PIGS IS PIGS AND OTHER FAVORITES, Ellis Parker Butler. The title story is one of the best humor short stories, as Mike Flannery obfuscates biology and English. Also included, That Pup of Murchison's, The Great American Pie Company, and Perkins of Portland. 14 illustrations. v + 109pp.   21532-6 Paperbound $1.00

THE PETERKIN PAPERS, Lucretia P. Hale. It takes genius to be as stupidly mad as the Peterkins, as they decide to become wise, celebrate the "Fourth," keep a cow, and otherwise strain the resources of the Lady from Philadelphia. Basic book of American humor. 153 illustrations. 219pp.   20794-3 Paperbound $1.50

PERRAULT'S FAIRY TALES, translated by A. E. Johnson and S. R. Littlewood, with 34 full-page illustrations by Gustave Doré. All the original Perrault stories—Cinderella, Sleeping Beauty, Bluebeard, Little Red Riding Hood, Puss in Boots, Tom Thumb, etc.—with their witty verse morals and the magnificent illustrations of Doré. One of the five or six great books of European fairy tales. viii + 117pp. 8⅛ x 11.   22311-6 Paperbound $2.00

OLD HUNGARIAN FAIRY TALES, Baroness Orczy. Favorites translated and adapted by author of the *Scarlet Pimpernel*. Eight fairy tales include "The Suitors of Princess Fire-Fly," "The Twin Hunchbacks," "Mr. Cuttlefish's Love Story," and "The Enchanted Cat." This little volume of magic and adventure will captivate children as it has for generations. 90 drawings by Montagu Barstow. 96pp.
(USO) 22293-4 Paperbound $1.95

THE RED FAIRY BOOK, Andrew Lang. Lang's color fairy books have long been children's favorites. This volume includes Rapunzel, Jack and the Bean-stalk and 35 other stories, familiar and unfamiliar. 4 plates, 93 illustrations x + 367pp.
21673-X Paperbound $2.50

THE BLUE FAIRY BOOK, Andrew Lang. Lang's tales come from all countries and all times. Here are 37 tales from Grimm, the Arabian Nights, Greek Mythology, and other fascinating sources. 8 plates, 130 illustrations. xi + 390pp.
21437-0 Paperbound $2.50

HOUSEHOLD STORIES BY THE BROTHERS GRIMM. Classic English-language edition of the well-known tales — Rumpelstiltskin, Snow White, Hansel and Gretel, The Twelve Brothers, Faithful John, Rapunzel, Tom Thumb (52 stories in all). Translated into simple, straightforward English by Lucy Crane. Ornamented with headpieces, vignettes, elaborate decorative initials and a dozen full-page illustrations by Walter Crane. x + 269pp.
21080-4 Paperbound $2.50

THE MERRY ADVENTURES OF ROBIN HOOD, Howard Pyle. The finest modern versions of the traditional ballads and tales about the great English outlaw. Howard Pyle's complete prose version, with every word, every illustration of the first edition. Do not confuse this facsimile of the original (1883) with modern editions that change text or illustrations. 23 plates plus many page decorations. xxii + 296pp.
22043-5 Paperbound $2.50

THE STORY OF KING ARTHUR AND HIS KNIGHTS, Howard Pyle. The finest children's version of the life of King Arthur; brilliantly retold by Pyle, with 48 of his most imaginative illustrations. xviii + 313pp. 6⅛ x 9¼.
21445-1 Paperbound $2.50

THE WONDERFUL WIZARD OF OZ, L. Frank Baum. America's finest children's book in facsimile of first edition with all Denslow illustrations in full color. The edition a child should have. Introduction by Martin Gardner. 23 color plates, scores of drawings. iv + 267pp.
20691-2 Paperbound $2.25

THE MARVELOUS LAND OF OZ, L. Frank Baum. The second Oz book, every bit as imaginative as the Wizard. The hero is a boy named Tip, but the Scarecrow and the Tin Woodman are back, as is the Oz magic. 16 color plates, 120 drawings by John R. Neill. 287pp.
20692-0 Paperbound $2.50

THE MAGICAL MONARCH OF MO, L. Frank Baum. Remarkable adventures in a land even stranger than Oz. The best of Baum's books not in the Oz series. 15 color plates and dozens of drawings by Frank Verbeck. xviii + 237pp.
21892-9 Paperbound $2.00

THE BAD CHILD'S BOOK OF BEASTS, MORE BEASTS FOR WORSE CHILDREN, A MORAL ALPHABET, Hilaire Belloc. Three complete humor classics in one volume. Be kind to the frog, and do not call him names . . . and 28 other whimsical animals. Familiar favorites and some not so well known. Illustrated by Basil Blackwell. 156pp.
(USO) 20749-8 Paperbound $1.25

EAST O' THE SUN AND WEST O' THE MOON, George W. Dasent. Considered the best of all translations of these Norwegian folk tales, this collection has been enjoyed by generations of children (and folklorists too). Includes True and Untrue, Why the Sea is Salt, East O' the Sun and West O' the Moon, Why the Bear is Stumpy-Tailed, Boots and the Troll, The Cock and the Hen, Rich Peter the Pedlar, and 52 more. The only edition with all 59 tales. 77 illustrations by Erik Werenskiold and Theodor Kittelsen. xv + 418pp. 22521-6 Paperbound $3.00

GOOPS AND HOW TO BE THEM, Gelett Burgess. Classic of tongue-in-cheek humor, masquerading as etiquette book. 87 verses, twice as many cartoons, show mischievous Goops as they demonstrate to children virtues of table manners, neatness, courtesy, etc. Favorite for generations. viii + 88pp. 6½ x 9¼.
22233-0 Paperbound $1.25

ALICE'S ADVENTURES UNDER GROUND, Lewis Carroll. The first version, quite different from the final *Alice in Wonderland*, printed out by Carroll himself with his own illustrations. Complete facsimile of the "million dollar" manuscript Carroll gave to Alice Liddell in 1864. Introduction by Martin Gardner. viii + 96pp. Title and dedication pages in color. 21482-6 Paperbound $1.25

THE BROWNIES, THEIR BOOK, Palmer Cox. Small as mice, cunning as foxes, exuberant and full of mischief, the Brownies go to the zoo, toy shop, seashore, circus, etc., in 24 verse adventures and 266 illustrations. Long a favorite, since their first appearance in St. Nicholas Magazine. xi + 144pp. 6⅝ x 9¼.
21265-3 Paperbound $1.75

SONGS OF CHILDHOOD, Walter De La Mare. Published (under the pseudonym Walter Ramal) when De La Mare was only 29, this charming collection has long been a favorite children's book. A facsimile of the first edition in paper, the 47 poems capture the simplicity of the nursery rhyme and the ballad, including such lyrics as I Met Eve, Tartary, The Silver Penny. vii + 106pp. 21972-0 Paperbound $1.25

THE COMPLETE NONSENSE OF EDWARD LEAR, Edward Lear. The finest 19th-century humorist-cartoonist in full: all nonsense limericks, zany alphabets, Owl and Pussycat, songs, nonsense botany, and more than 500 illustrations by Lear himself. Edited by Holbrook Jackson. xxix + 287pp. (USO) 20167-8 Paperbound $2.00

BILLY WHISKERS: THE AUTOBIOGRAPHY OF A GOAT, Frances Trego Montgomery. A favorite of children since the early 20th century, here are the escapades of that rambunctious, irresistible and mischievous goat—Billy Whiskers. Much in the spirit of *Peck's Bad Boy*, this is a book that children never tire of reading or hearing. All the original familiar illustrations by W. H. Fry are included: 6 color plates, 18 black and white drawings. 159pp. 22345-0 Paperbound $2.00

MOTHER GOOSE MELODIES. Faithful republication of the fabulously rare Munroe and Francis "copyright 1833" Boston edition—the most important Mother Goose collection, usually referred to as the "original." Familiar rhymes plus many rare ones, with wonderful old woodcut illustrations. Edited by E. F. Bleiler. 128pp. 4½ x 6⅜. 22577-1 Paperbound $1.25

Two Little Savages; Being the Adventures of Two Boys Who Lived as Indians and What They Learned, Ernest Thompson Seton. Great classic of nature and boyhood provides a vast range of woodlore in most palatable form, a genuinely entertaining story. Two farm boys build a teepee in woods and live in it for a month, working out Indian solutions to living problems, star lore, birds and animals, plants, etc. 293 illustrations. vii + 286pp.

20985-7 Paperbound $2.50

Peter Piper's Practical Principles of Plain & Perfect Pronunciation. Alliterative jingles and tongue-twisters of surprising charm, that made their first appearance in America about 1830. Republished in full with the spirited woodcut illustrations from this earliest American edition. 32pp. 4½ x 6⅜.

22560-7 Paperbound $1.00

Science Experiments and Amusements for Children, Charles Vivian. 73 easy experiments, requiring only materials found at home or easily available, such as candles, coins, steel wool, etc.; illustrate basic phenomena like vacuum, simple chemical reaction, etc. All safe. Modern, well-planned. Formerly *Science Games for Children.* 102 photos, numerous drawings. 96pp. 6⅛ x 9¼.

21856-2 Paperbound $1.25

An Introduction to Chess Moves and Tactics Simply Explained, Leonard Barden. Informal intermediate introduction, quite strong in explaining reasons for moves. Covers basic material, tactics, important openings, traps, positional play in middle game, end game. Attempts to isolate patterns and recurrent configurations. Formerly *Chess.* 58 figures. 102pp.   (USO) 21210-6 Paperbound $1.25

Lasker's Manual of Chess, Dr. Emanuel Lasker. Lasker was not only one of the five great World Champions, he was also one of the ablest expositors, theorists, and analysts. In many ways, his Manual, permeated with his philosophy of battle, filled with keen insights, is one of the greatest works ever written on chess. Filled with analyzed games by the great players. A single-volume library that will profit almost any chess player, beginner or master. 308 diagrams. xli x 349pp.

20640-8 Paperbound $2.75

The Master Book of Mathematical Recreations, Fred Schuh. In opinion of many the finest work ever prepared on mathematical puzzles, stunts, recreations; exhaustively thorough explanations of mathematics involved, analysis of effects, citation of puzzles and games. Mathematics involved is elementary. Translated by F. Göbel. 194 figures. xxiv + 430pp.   22134-2 Paperbound $3.00

Mathematics, Magic and Mystery, Martin Gardner. Puzzle editor for Scientific American explains mathematics behind various mystifying tricks: card tricks, stage "mind reading," coin and match tricks, counting out games, geometric dissections, etc. Probability sets, theory of numbers clearly explained. Also provides more than 400 tricks, guaranteed to work, that you can do. 135 illustrations. xii + 176pp.

20338-2 Paperbound $1.50

MATHEMATICAL PUZZLES FOR BEGINNERS AND ENTHUSIASTS, Geoffrey Mott-Smith. 189 puzzles from easy to difficult—involving arithmetic, logic, algebra, properties of digits, probability, etc.—for enjoyment and mental stimulus. Explanation of mathematical principles behind the puzzles. 135 illustrations. viii + 248pp.
20198-8 Paperbound $1.75

PAPER FOLDING FOR BEGINNERS, William D. Murray and Francis J. Rigney. Easiest book on the market, clearest instructions on making interesting, beautiful origami. Sail boats, cups, roosters, frogs that move legs, bonbon boxes, standing birds, etc. 40 projects; more than 275 diagrams and photographs. 94pp.
20713-7 Paperbound $1.00

TRICKS AND GAMES ON THE POOL TABLE, Fred Herrmann. 79 tricks and games—some solitaires, some for two or more players, some competitive games—to entertain you between formal games. Mystifying shots and throws, unusual caroms, tricks involving such props as cork, coins, a hat, etc. Formerly *Fun on the Pool Table*. 77 figures. 95pp.
21814-7 Paperbound $1.00

HAND SHADOWS TO BE THROWN UPON THE WALL: A SERIES OF NOVEL AND AMUSING FIGURES FORMED BY THE HAND, Henry Bursill. Delightful picturebook from great-grandfather's day shows how to make 18 different hand shadows: a bird that flies, duck that quacks, dog that wags his tail, camel, goose, deer, boy, turtle, etc. Only book of its sort. vi + 33pp. 6½ x 9¼.
21779-5 Paperbound $1.00

WHITTLING AND WOODCARVING, E. J. Tangerman. 18th printing of best book on market. "If you can cut a potato you can carve" toys and puzzles, chains, chessmen, caricatures, masks, frames, woodcut blocks, surface patterns, much more. Information on tools, woods, techniques. Also goes into serious wood sculpture from Middle Ages to present, East and West. 464 photos, figures. x + 293pp.
20965-2 Paperbound $2.00

HISTORY OF PHILOSOPHY, Julián Marias. Possibly the clearest, most easily followed, best planned, most useful one-volume history of philosophy on the market; neither skimpy nor overfull. Full details on system of every major philosopher and dozens of less important thinkers from pre-Socratics up to Existentialism and later. Strong on many European figures usually omitted. Has gone through dozens of editions in Europe. 1966 edition, translated by Stanley Appelbaum and Clarence Strowbridge. xviii + 505pp.
21739-6 Paperbound $3.00

YOGA: A SCIENTIFIC EVALUATION, Kovoor T. Behanan. Scientific but non-technical study of physiological results of yoga exercises; done under auspices of Yale U. Relations to Indian thought, to psychoanalysis, etc. 16 photos. xxiii + 270pp.
20505-3 Paperbound $2.50

Prices subject to change without notice.
Available at your book dealer or write for free catalogue to Dept. GI, Dover Publications, Inc., 180 Varick St., N. Y., N. Y. 10014. Dover publishes more than 150 books each year on science, elementary and advanced mathematics, biology, music, art, literary history, social sciences and other areas.

Date Due

APR 22 '74		
FEB 4 '76		
REPAIR		
MR 28 '78		